Ripples from Carcosa

Ripples from Carcosa
H. P. Lovecraft, Haunted Landscapes, and *True Detective*

Heather Miller

Hippocampus Press

New York

Copyright © 2024 by Heather Miller

Published by Hippocampus Press
P.O. Box 641, New York, NY 10156.
www.hippocampuspress.com
All rights reserved.

No part of this work may be reproduced in any form or by any means without the written permission of the publisher.

Cover art and design by Daniel V. Sauer, dansauerdesign.com.
Hippocampus Press logo designed by Anastasia Damianakos.

First Edition
1 3 5 7 9 8 6 4 2
ISBN: 978-1-61498-447-4

Contents

Preface 7

Introduction: The America of *True Detective* 9

Chapter 1: Haunted Landscapes, Haunted People 11

Chapter 2: The Tatters of *The King* 29

Chapter 3: Thomas Ligotti and the Unreliability of Human Understanding 47

Chapter 4: Signposts in H. P. Lovecraft toward *True Detective* and an
    Aesthetics of Investigation 61

Chapter 5: H. P. Lovecraft and the Dynamics of Detective Fiction 79

Chapter 6: The Weird within the Real: Common Territories in Lovecraft's
    Fiction and Southern Literature 99

Chapter 7: *True Detective,* Lovecraft, and the Cult of the Yellow King 113

Appendix: *True Detective* Season 1 Cast 127

Works Cited 129

Index 137

Preface

In preparing this text, I have chosen to observe some textual conventions for the sake of ease of reading and writing. One of those involves the tricky nature of referring to The King in Yellow. We must keep four related things in mind. There are:

- The King in Yellow, the figure referenced in the play *The King in Yellow* and in numerous works by others
- The *King in Yellow,* the play cited in Chambers/created by Chambers and subsequently insinuated into numerous works by others
- The Cult of the Yellow King, the cult in *True Detective* with connections to Chambers's works through folk horror
- The Yellow King, the name in *True Detective* found in Dora Lange's diary and mentioned by multiple characters; parallel to Chambers's *King in Yellow*

The easy elision among these concepts reflects the nature and spirit of the Yellow King—his decadence, his absorption of all human life, the ease and willingness with which humans embrace him, and perhaps ultimately his artistic nature and his status as Art itself, unfiltered by any mediating experience. The present study embraces a particular set of textual conventions concerning Chambers, his book, the play he mentions, and the figure of the Yellow King. Herein, the book written by Chambers, *The King in Yellow*, is styled as "the Book." The play *The King in Yellow* is styled as "the Play." The figure both within the Play and that cited in *True Detective* is styled as "the Yellow King."[1]

Textually speaking, in addition to the styling of Chambers's work as set above, I have chosen to employ the following additional conventions:

---

1. These conventions I gleefully borrow, with heartfelt thanks, from M. Grant Kellermeyer's annotated edition of *The King in Yellow* (Fort Wayne, IN: Oldstyle Tales Press, 2016).

- Gothic rather than gothic, except when in a direct quotation
- South rather than south when referring to the southeastern United States
- Season and episode citation of *True Detective* as, for example, S1E1 to represent season 1, episode 1

And there are some topics that, because they are better and more thoroughly discussed by others, I address only briefly here:

- Media studies and media history
- Film studies and film history
- Race, gender, and class theory
- Colonialism, post-colonialism, and the post/colonial subject
- Queer theory and queer studies
- Any number of other subjects that are common currency at the time of this writing

My work here is limited to an examination of Lovecraft in the context of *True Detective* season 1 and a handful of associated thinkers. A great deal of careful, important research has been published in the areas listed above. I recommend that the reader pursue the specialists in those fields for fuller, more rewarding reading on those topics.

I use the following abbreviations in the text:

CE   Lovecraft, *Collected Essays* (2004–06)
CF   Lovecraft, *Collected Fiction: A Variorum Edition* (2015–17)

Introduction: The America of *True Detective*

> It is *because* the cosmos is meaningless that we must secure our individual illusions of values, direction, and interest by upholding the artificial streams which give us such worlds of salutary illusion. That is—since nothing means anything in itself, we must preserve the proximate and arbitrary background which makes things around us seem as if they did mean something.
> —H. P. Lovecraft, *Letters to James F. Morton,* 243

In the America of *True Detective,* things are never as simple as they seem. This is equally true for the New England of H. P. Lovecraft, the Yoknapatawpha County of William Faulkner, the New York and Paris of Robert W. Chambers in *The King in Yellow,* the many locales of Edgar Allan Poe, and the southern Louisiana of Richard Misrach and Kate Orff's *Petrochemical America*. In pursuit of truth and justice, or at least a criminal, and after excavating layers of misdirection designed to confuse the culprit's identity and obscure his guilt, corruption, graft, mendacity, and any combination of mortal sins the culprit has committed, the detective may find that underneath each layer is not the truth, but instead yet another strategy of concealment. Instead of turtles all the way down, he sees more lies.

What are we to do when we conclude that we cannot trust what we're told? What do we do when we're haunted by the histories of our homes, our towns and cities, our families, our countries? What do we draw on for strength and a sense of self when history becomes a spectre? These questions often go unrecognized in the American narrative for several reasons: the impulse to optimism, as Thomas Ligotti would be quick to point out; the national impulse to dismiss intellectual pursuits in favor of the rough-and-ready manhandling of life and its difficulties; a generalized mistrust of anything that seems European and thus weak or feminine.

As William Faulkner reminds us, the past isn't even the past, and these questions return again and again. The protagonists in Lovecraft, Chambers, and *True Detective* wrestle with their distrust of the present and phantoms from the past. In this book I examine fiction, narrative, and history, with threads teased out for areas of interest as they can be traced back to the central question. The spine of my work is built around J. Hillis Miller's important essay on narrative and history, with this question to answer:

Given Edgar Allan Poe, detective fiction, Southern literature (especially Southern Gothic and the grotesque), aesthetics, epistemology, Thomas Ligotti's sense of conspiracy, the art and craft of investigation, Ambrose Bierce, Robert W. Chambers, Carcosa and the King in Yellow (the book, the play, and the figure), tropes, figures, and the weird, how is it that only H. P. Lovecraft can pull all these threads, and more, together? How is it that without Lovecraft, *True Detective* season 1 could not have existed?

This book goes both broadly and deeply. Broadly: Lovecraft, detective fiction, Southern literature, aesthetics, epistemology, the grotesque, palimpsests, Thomas Ligotti, Ambrose Bierce, tabletop role-playing games, the Dhammapada, Sir Arthur Conan Doyle, masking, violence and the sacred, normative values, criminality, tropes in multiple genres, and *True Detective*—and that is an overview rather than a deep dive.

Deeply: to get at the broad topics, I approach them from the points of view of epistemology, aesthetics, and abjection, with the argument that in the particular way that Lovecraft, detective fiction, and Southern literature are brought together in *True Detective*, we cannot easily disentangle epistemology, aesthetics, and abjection from one another, and the three lead us to the grotesque rather than away from it. I bring these ideas together through haunting, the haunted, and haunted landscapes. Although I discuss tropes a great deal in the context of detective fiction and focus on revelation and concealment as the master trope of that genre, the tension between "haunting" and "the haunted" is arguably the master trope within which the other ideas and tropes here function.

But how does it fit together? Miller's essay examines the relationships that narrative has to historical texts through the lens of deconstruction. In addition, I take from Gary Budden and David Southwell some ideas from landscape punk and wed them to the work done by Richard Misrach and Kate Orff in their book *Petrochemical America*. Along with support from other ideas, these become the core concept of the haunted landscape, where I examine Lovecraft and *True Detective*, demonstrating the necessity of Lovecraft's vision for the existence of *True Detective*. Without Lovecraft, *True Detective* season 1—and implicitly the subsequent seasons—could not have come about.

Chapter 1: Haunted Landscapes, Haunted People

> Some heads are more haunted than others, whether they are haunted by ghosts or by gods or by creatures from outer space.
> —Thomas Ligotti, *Teatro Grottesco*

The longer America exists, the more haunted it becomes.

Once an Eden, a place of innocence where European refugees escaping religious persecution could find a new start,[1] America soon found its own dark Gothic heart in its swamps and antebellum mansions. Its witches may not have been burned alive, but persecutions and incarcerations formed a deep, rich vein of activity for the powerful to use against others. The European Gothic became the American Gothic, then the Southern Gothic, and through it all were the hauntings.

American history, with its register of victims both named and nameless, could not have been anything less than haunted. On a landscape already bloodied by wars among Native American tribes before the arrival of Europeans, the conflicts brought by those Europeans were more than an accelerant—but this is a discussion that is far too large for this study to cover. What is important to note is that one context for American history is its haunted landscape, that is, the remnants of its history that remind those in the present of the *truth* of that history. This haunted landscape bears witness to and for the past.

Landscape dominates the present study. Its linkages to the past, to history, to personal and political place, to time and events, and to narrative make it inescapable. Rather than being a passive context for the actions of humans, in this study landscape is an active participant and a commentary on multiple levels. It

---

1. I offer this as an introductory perspective on American history not because it is current—it is no longer widely taught in schools—but because as an idea it, too, is now part of the haunted landscape of American history.

is a determining factor in numerous stories in Lovecraft's oeuvre; it is a critical factor as the urban environment in Chambers's book; and it is an additional cast member in *True Detective* even as it is a site of personal, political, and environmental contest in the very real world of south Louisiana.

Landscape is inescapable, pressing, almost determinative. It is both the obstacle and the way. It provides initial context, then comes to dominate the narrative. Through humanity's actions, it changes from nurturer to poisoner. Far from being an easily dismissed matter of poetic description or pseudo-romantic reflection of character, landscape reminds us that there is no escape. In some ways, landscape may be the ultimate reminder that man cannot escape who and what he is.

Landscape studies in literature, i.e., investigations into the ways landscape interacts with narrative, is a burgeoning area of literary investigation. Interestingly, some have linked landscape studies to deconstruction, noting that "landscape . . . carries a relational hybridity, always already natural and cultural, deep and superficial, which makes for something inherently deconstructive" (Matless, cited in Heholt and Downing 6). Nowhere is the concept of the always already, the *toujours-déjà* of 1990s cultural critique, made clearer than in the relationship of the southern United States to its landscape. As William Faulkner wrote in *Requiem for a Nun,* "The past is never dead. It's not even past" (85). For Southerners of many ethnicities, the landscape of the South is the *always* of the past mated with the *already* of the present, a present squirming in the grip of the past.

The effects of Southern history are hard and inescapable. Not only has the slave trade of the West and the wreckage of nineteenth- and twentieth-century American history had profound effects and consequences for all those in the South, the general resistance to change and the necessary incrementalism that resulted has meant that much of the South has remained a world apart. The South both participates in and stands to the side of American history. One foot in its history—all its history—and one foot on the unsteady terrain of modernity, the South cannot be in the present yet cannot remain in its past.

As a consequence, the literature of the South—long dominated by white writers until roughly the mid to late twentieth century—reflects this awareness of its uncertain state. A people aware of themselves as both walled within their own history and set on the margins of the history of the American project by virtue of having lost a civil war, Southerners have turned to their landscapes of battlefields, statues, plantations and plantation houses, cemeteries, and centuries-old cities founded well before America in search of a context for themselves and a figuration of some kind of place in time and history.

This first principle of place, or as Eudora Welty and other writers have described it, a "sense of place," can also be found in Lovecraft, as I discuss in chapter 6. Briefly, Lovecraft (often, though not exclusively) uses the New England landscape as the context for his examination of cosmic horror, giving cosmic horror the critically necessary context of the real that he insisted was essential for cosmic horror to have its fullest expression (*CE* 2.116). What does it take for a landscape to be haunted, at least for the purposes of this study? And how is the haunting in this way conveyed to the people who inhabit a given landscape?

First, we will need to address the difference between "ghosts" and "haunting." Here I will not use "ghosts" in the service of the trope of "haunting." Ghosts as the inhabitants of a landscape certainly serve a purpose, but as the shades of individuals, with all that entails—personal histories, remnants of personalities, murky motives, and other possible characteristics—ghosts are an aspect of a landscape without necessarily being integrated into the landscape. That is, ghosts foreground themselves onto the background of the landscape they haunt. Ghosts add a layer of obscuration onto a landscape that probably already conveys a complex history. Ghosts are a layer of information, difficult to understand in terms of significance and at the very least off-putting, yet at the same time they function as a palimpsest, a topic and term discussed in chapter 5. For those interested in landscape, however, ghosts are a distraction.

Without ghosts, then, how can a landscape be considered haunted? This form of haunting arises from multiple aspects, not the least of which is the particulars of its history. Landscape is haunted by the past actions of the very alive humans who once inhabited it. These actions, past leading into present, form the psychosphere of a location, as Rustin Cohle describes it in S1E1 of *True Detective*, "The Long Bright Dark": "I get a bad taste in my mouth out here. Aluminum. Ash. I can smell the psychosphere." The aluminum and ash that Cohle tastes arise from the chemical plants that line a section of the Mississippi River between Baton Rouge and New Orleans that is colloquially known as "Cancer Alley." Cancer Alley is a classic example of a haunted landscape: a place defined by activities that linger, unseen yet with ongoing effects on its inhabitants, and with its inhabitants' full awareness. A haunted landscape is defined by its edges;

these edges are formed by events rather than maps. The patterns, emotions, and residues of the past and present reverberate through a haunted landscape.

This reverberation is strongly present in both Lovecraft and *True Detective*. In Lovecraft's fiction, we see time and again a landscape that bears witness to aeons-old activities by vast alien beings. Most strikingly, the vast, Cyclopean city in *At the Mountains of Madness* (1931) offers the reader (and Lovecraft's scientists) a haunted landscape the reveals its history even as the living, present-day creatures inhabiting it, descendants of ancient scientific experiments, threaten the investigators (*CF* 3.11–157). In turn, the investigators, the evolved descendants of some of these creatures that were created in jest, confront both the historical record and the historical consequence. This combination of record and consequence provides the outlines of a haunted landscape.

In *True Detective,* the landscape is essentially a character without a listing in the credits. Its power and force accompany Rustin Cohle and Martin Hart as they investigate, claim success, then disintegrate as police detectives only to reintegrate as, in Cohle's case, a private citizen, and, in Hart's case, a private investigator. Their respective personal histories haunt them; the long history of deceit and exploitation in the South in general and southern Louisiana in particular is the haunting of the physical landscape Cohle and Hart live and work in; and the present-day, specific criminal exploitation, abuse, and murder of children and youths in the immediate area around Interstate 10 in southern Louisiana is another haunting of both people and landscape. As with Faulkner's quotation about the past, this haunting—these hauntings—are inescapable.

With the above in mind, we can see the beginning traces of H. P. Lovecraft's use of human history versus cosmic indifference as the landscape for cosmic horror, as well as detective fiction's couching of the genre's tropes within various landscapes such as the British country manor mystery, the American hard-boiled urban environment, and even nineteenth-century British cityscapes and landscapes. All these ideas will be discussed later in this text.

Rather than simply being populated by ghosts, the narratives I examine here offer landscapes that themselves populate the narratives and consciousness of the characters. In Robert W. Chambers's work *The King in Yellow* (1895), the landscape of Carcosa begins to intrude upon the real-life world of Hildred Castaigne, the main character of the story "The Repairer of Reputations." As some critics have noted (see, e.g., notes in Hite and Kellermeyer editions of

Chambers), Castaigne is no doubt insane on some level, yet throughout the Book, Carcosa inserts itself into reality once a given character reads the Play. My take on the Book, which I explain more fully in chapter 2, is that Carcosa has an agency as a landscape that blurs the lines between readers of the Play and the landscape of Carcosa, effectively making the old landscape of the reader be replaced by Carcosa itself, in an ultimate act of hegemony and expatriation. Castaigne is in a haunted landscape, but might it be a landscape under transformation by Carcosa and the Yellow King? It is possible that Castaigne's landscape suffers the effects of Carcosa's initial intrusions into the reality that the other characters inhabit, so that what is to others Castaigne's insanity is for Castaigne simply reality—an accurate representation of place.

Given that a haunted landscape depends on multiple modalities, including the physical context of Cohle's psychosphere, it will profit us to discuss briefly what is referred to as "place." One of the genre elements often cited concerning Southern literature is its sense of place, a matter I link to Lovecraft's fiction in chapter 6. With regard to haunted landscapes, as Heholt and Downing observe,

> [W]e need both the specificities of a place as well as the specificities of experience. The term 'haunting' echoes a multiplicity of meanings and experiences, from the directly phenomenological, to visions of ghosts, the trace hauntings of trauma or remnants of the past. Hauntings are multiple *and* specific; there are hauntings, plural but particular. (13)

Although I do not address ghosts in this study, the importance of trauma, the past, and history cannot be overstated. Place, space, and landscape are all factors linking Chambers's text, Lovecraft's stories, and *True Detective,* with the emotionally haunting effects of history and the past affecting the characters in radical ways. The Play haunts the characters in Chambers's Yellow stories, and contact with it opens the path for Carcosa's incursions into everyday reality. For Lovecraft, human history is for naught in the face of cosmic indifference, including, and perhaps especially, that of his beloved New England. The bulk of human history is swatted away by the weight of cosmic powers for whom humans barely register. In *True Detective,* the full weight of Southern history and its present-day dynamics forms the context of the investigation into the cult of the Yellow King and the murders of young, desperate people in southern Louisiana.

Lovecraft renders landscapes impossible for his protagonists. The thick ice of Antarctica, the oceans of the south Pacific, the menacing streets of Red Hook, and other settings conspire against the characters traversing them. At the same time, those landscapes turn the revelations presented to the characters into life-changing events. Lovecraft's haunted landscapes are a direct link to *True Detective*. Chambers provides the key trope of the Yellow King as a form of folklore threading through the narrative of *True Detective;* Thomas Ligotti provides Cohle's pessimistic worldview; but Lovecraft provides the spine along which the various tropes and ideas are connected.

Yet there are more ways to approach these ideas. Gary Budden picked up the term "landscape punk" from David Southwell, the author who created Hookland, a psychogeographic locale and creative experiment. As an exercise in psychogeography,[2] Hookland brings together the do-it-yourself ethos of writers in general, tropes from landscape fiction, and weird fiction. As Southwell notes,

> Folklore is part of our conversation with land. A way of seeing ourselves in the narrative of place. It is our access to the psychic shrapnel of event, embedded around us. This is our line of transmission. It is echo memory. It is fault line. Folklore is narrative constantly cheating death by changing its jacket. Folklore is the liar that tells the truth of soil, of place. (Hookland)

Although this study does not dive into folklore, it is worth noting here that Chambers's *The King in Yellow* provides the folklore that is necessary for the plot of season 1 of *True Detective*. Behind the Yellow King are Lovecraft's haunted landscapes, giving everything else a place to inhabit even as those haunted landscapes represent a high degree of epistemological disorder for those trying to navigate them.

One of the core principles of landscape punk is the layering of history in a given locale. Whereas in America those layers are in the early stage of development, in Europe we see a much richer palimpsest of historical layering. Budden notes that "[t]hat sense of layers, of history so dense it became intimidating to pick apart, was drilled into me. The sense that there might just be more to life, to reality, than our individual experiences" ("Awake"). We see this happening in *True Detective* through the overt images of petrochemical factories and

---

2. Psychogeography is "the exploration of urban environments that emphasizes interpersonal connections to places and arbitrary routes, and follows a loosely defined urban practice known as the dérive" (Wikipedia). Psychogeography and its associated ideas are recommended to the reader as a rich vein of investigation.

the covert, implied layering of history through such plot elements as Courir de Mardi Gras, a spring celebration in rural Louisiana that stretches back to the earliest Mardi Gras celebrations and which originated in fifteenth-century France (Bradshaw). In *True Detective,* the context of the area murders and the generalized menace posed by the power structures in the South make what might have been relatively innocent play into something much darker, something that carries the taint of history, American history and Southern history both.

The stories in both Lovecraft and *True Detective* would be impossible without, perhaps inevitable with, those landscapes. Behind the landscapes lie darker forces, forces larger than the humans inhabiting them.

Similarly, *Petrochemical America,* a photography book that is also a data-driven examination of the development and consequences of Cancer Alley in southern Louisiana, presents landscapes that are impossible for humans to inhabit safely. The authors show us a world where larger-than-life forces—in this case, petrochemical manufacturers—have imposed landscapes on the inhabiting humans that they cannot influence without extreme effort and which lead to conflict, disease, and death. These people inhabit a world changed by a seeping, poisonous presence, and they are equally changed by it.

Importantly, *Petrochemical America* also provides critical imagery for *True Detective*. The opening credits for each episode of season 1 use multiple images from the book, over which are laid the main figures and important illustrative scenes from the episodes. The land and landscape of southern Louisiana are the backdrop of ruin, waste, and death. The landscape is tainted by the present and grayed by the past, haunted by the actions of the people who have possessed that land. Possession of the land and landscape has poison and profit as its consequences. The land becomes an impossible site to inhabit, even as those living there are trapped by the economies of power and profit.

In an oddly parallel way, the *Delta Green* game *Impossible Landscapes,* a tabletop role-playing game, offers a world that is being encroached upon—and physically altered by—the growing influence and infiltration of Carcosa and the Yellow King. Briefly, *Impossible Landscapes* brings the Delta Green agents into missions—a series of five—that lead them closer to Carcosa, a malevolent dream world outside normal reality and that is the "home" of the Yellow King. As the agents investigate, their resolve weakens and sanity lessens until they are of necessity in Carcosa itself, struggling to release our reality from the grasp of the Yellow King. The players find themselves battling their own changing psychological and physical states even as they go up against malevolent forces intent on manifesting Carcosa in our world. For now, let us examine how Lovecraft's landscapes make possible the impossible landscapes of Dennis Detwiller's work and others and presage the landscape punk of *Petrochemical America*. We will need to begin with an important essay from a key deconstructionist.

The literary critic J. Hillis Miller published the essay "Narrative and History" in 1974 when he was part of the Yale School of deconstruction, where he researched Victorian and Modernist literature. "Narrative and History" leans toward Miller's interests in Modernism. Given Heholt and Downing's attention to deconstruction as an approach to understanding the pluralities of haunted landscapes, chiefly for my interests here is how Miller discusses reading as a cultural act, that is, the way that a given set of words, as a text, can be connected to other texts through a kind of nested relationship of texts-within-texts (Miller, "The Critic" 443–44), or, if you will, how texts haunt other texts from within.

Miller begins "Narrative and History" with an examination of how fiction is presented as an act of deceit: "a work of fiction is conventionally presented not as a work of fiction but as some other form of language. This is almost always some "representational" form rooted in history and in the direct report of 'real' human experience" (456). Miller describes a text disguising itself as another text in order to represent its stance from a different rhetorical place. In other words, the "original" rhetorical place/situation/stance haunts the "represented" rhetorical stance. The work of fiction represents itself as a report of some authorial or narrative voice, sometimes a character (who is presented as a "real" person, itself a haunting) who exists and acts within a "real" place for the purpose of making a point about life, human nature, or the like. What happens beneath all this sleight-of-hand is the haunting of the representation of the "real"—a place that exists as presented only in the fictional work—by the reality of the fiction, that is to say, the work of fiction exists within the representation of the real as a vestige of an existence within the representation. It is perhaps necessary for this kind of haunting that realism, in its traditional literary sense, be employed, i.e., a kind of representational fiction that is not necessarily avant garde or otherwise on a given stylistic or generic edge.[3] Either way,

---

3. Arguments could be made otherwise that would be better suited for research

realism and its conventions give the idea of a haunting credence because they establish the context for the ghostly material inhabiting its boundaries to exist.

Lovecraft's insistence on the importance of realism to make the weird seem plausible becomes important here. For Lovecraft, the weird is cloaked in the real. What for other writers might be a genre convention becomes the critical context that makes Lovecraft's use of cosmic horror so effective and is what ultimately lends credence to his larger message about human insignificance. The real does not contain the weird so much as it offers an atmosphere within which the weird may breed. The weird isn't so weird without the real, and in this way we can posit that the weird haunts the real.

Miller describes the act of writing as displacement (456), where the author "becomes" characters, the characters "become" figures with lives, thoughts, feelings, desires, and motives that existed before the narrative they inhabit and which will ostensibly exist after (unless a given figure or figures experience "death," which the authors must concoct and the narrator present). These, too, are hauntings, where the "author"—a rhetorical stance that does not completely capture or represent the agent who writes—haunts the characters, the characters haunt the narrative, the narrative haunts the reader, the reader carries the revenants. Miller's realism is one of layers of mapped description overlaid onto a reality that is constantly being reinterpreted. The difficulty with this map is the instability of both it and its corresponding territory:

> This reversal or suppression of the displacement involved in writing a work of fiction takes several forms. A novel may present itself as a collection of letters . . . as memoirs or edited documents . . . as an old manuscript found in a trunk or bottle . . . as an autobiography . . . as a legal deposition . . . as journalism . . . as a travel book . . . or even as a realistic painting. (456–57)

This instability is ripe for any number of critical approaches, but especially deconstruction. Deconstructionists note that representation is impossible in some sense; it must always settle for being an approximation (Burleson 1–3).[4] Conventional wisdom, at least as offered in conventional classes on the writing of fiction, claims that concealing the author's efforts is somehow related to the

---

outside the scope of this work.
4. These pages serve as a starter, but in fact, the entire first chapter of Burleson's book is a solid introduction to deconstruction.

skill and guile of the author. The better the author's efforts are concealed, the better the author's skill and guile.

This position has been critiqued, of course, yet it seems to remain part of the core, and perhaps most conservative, definition of realism. Deconstruction questions this definition by pointing out the oppositions and tensions found in a work and exposing the concealed structures and assumptions. Miller was one of the twentieth century's notable deconstructionists, so we can expect to find deconstructionist techniques in his essay. Here, Miller's characterization of this rhetorical strategy as "masking" (457) leads him to point to the authorial strategy of dismissing the term "fiction" by instead using terms such as "history," which turns the reader toward ideas such as fact, truth, accuracy, and reality (457). Whereas Miller discusses this strategy in terms of anxiety, concealment, and constraint (457), we can describe it again as a haunting, except here the author is haunted by what Miller calls "gratuitousness . . . baseless creativity and lie" (457). Claiming "verisimilitude" (457) allows the author to reduce the anxiety and instead affirm, according to Henry James, "himself as a historian and his narrative as history" (James 59; Miller 458). Displacement, deferral, and Lacanian sleight-of-hand abound.[5]

Ultimately, Miller's—and deconstruction's—project is to go about unmasking the masked, unraveling the woven, unseating the comfortable. As Burleson notes in his discussion of how post-structuralism made its predecessor structuralism uneasy,

---

5. We can find numerous examples of these strategies in Lovecraft, who uses, among other devices, letters in numerous stories. Memoirs or edited documents show up in "The Whisperer in Darkness"; "The Call of Cthulhu" involves an old manuscript found in a trunk as well as journalism in the form of newspaper articles. "The Shadow out of Time" engages matters of autobiography and self-understanding, and "The Thing on the Doorstep" involves a legal deposition. *At the Mountains of Madness* is a combination of travelogue and scientific report. And were it not for the paintings of "Pickman's Model," the narrator may have never learned the truth about Pickman's activities. Lovecraft's insistence on the use of verisimilitude as the defining context for the weird means that his fiction's associations with history are inevitable. Lovecraft detaches his narratives from mundane human history and reattaches them to the reality behind that history, which then becomes a natural history of the weird.

[o]ne approach that deconstructive reading takes is to demonstrate, in the text, that within each term of the binary opposition the other term secretly and necessarily dwells. If the opposition is "x versus y" then x contains a y-aspect that must be there in order for x to function as x, and y contains an x-aspect that must be there in order for y to function as y. Thus the differences operative in the text are not so much a matter of x's difference from y as they are a matter of x's difference from x and y's difference from y. Neither term is "self-identical" or indivisibly characterizable. (7)

Deconstruction takes particular delight in showing how the critical approaches of previous generations can be unraveled the same way a fictional narrative can, and detective fiction's tropes inevitably came under its scrutiny (see, e.g., a simple Google Scholar search for "deconstruction and detective fiction," which returns publications so numerous as to escape easy compilation). What is most applicable for this study is Miller's calling out of the self-effacing strategies in the novel (456), and how the ideas of fiction writing, masking, and realism work together not only in Miller's essay but also in Lovecraft and *True Detective* to create a sense of haunting and the haunted.

For Miller, masking is the effort of the author to shift attention away from himself as an author and from his text as a work of fiction (457). As an effort at misdirection, masking intends as its goal the encouragement of the reader's complicity with the author's strategies (after all, what else is suspension of disbelief but self-deceit?). This strategy asks the reader to alter how he knows what he knows—to make an epistemological shift—and, accordingly, to adjust his perceptions of the conventions and skill employed by the author—to make an aesthetic shift.

By employing both epistemology and aesthetics in the examination of the act of masking, Miller illuminates a path through the numerous areas in this study. Briefly—a point to be discussed more fully later—a haunted landscape and a haunted narrative both require the device of the mask in order for the unmasking to take place and the revelations of the haunting to come about. The chain of masks worn begins with language itself—language being the mediator between reality and how we communicate with others and ourselves; then we move to the author's mask, then the mask of realism as "actual" representation, then the mask of narrative as an "actual" representation of "events," then the mask of fiction itself, which becomes the mask seen by the reader, who resides behind his own layers of masks acquired throughout his life.

The struggle to remove these masks is at the core of both Chambers's *The King in Yellow* and *True Detective*. The characters are haunted by the realities that they believe to be true and that are in conflict with what they see going on around them. Some of the victims in *True Detective* have been told about The Yellow King—the murder victim Dora Lange has a diary filled with notes, chants, and drawings of him, for example—and the characters in Chambers's Yellow stories struggle to retain their grip on reality after they read the Play. The masks these characters once wore have been changed; they now know the world is different, yet they cannot reconcile themselves with this new knowledge.

In "Narrative and History," Miller focuses on two authors: Henry James and George Eliot. He states about James, "It is impossible to imagine what a novelist takes himself to be unless he regards himself as a historian and his narrative as history . . . to insert into his attempt a back-bone of logic, he must relate events that are assumed to be real" (458). Later, he notes, "The substantiality of 'the most solid story-tellers' depends on having a 'somewhere', an assumed historical reality as a background or scene . . . [the] metonymic transfer which is the basis of all narrative" (459). Lovecraft understands the importance of providing realism as the "somewhere" that precedes the weird and its reader of weird fiction with associated cosmic horror. As he writes in his essay "Notes on Writing Weird Fiction" (1933),

> Inconceivable events and conditions have a special handicap to overcome, and this can be accomplished only through the maintenance of a careful realism in every phase of the story except that touching on the one given marvel. This marvel must be treated very impressively and deliberately—with a careful emotional "build-up"—else it will seem flat and unconvincing. Being the principal thing in the story, its mere existence should overshadow the characters and events. But the characters and events must be consistent and natural except where they touch the single marvel. In relation to the central wonder, the characters should shew the same overwhelming emotion which similar characters would shew toward such a wonder in real life. Never have a wonder taken for granted. (*CE* 2.177)

Although Miller does not mention Lovecraft, he might as well have. Lovecraft's rhetorical strategy of nesting the weird within the real—of letting the weird haunt the real—is one and the same as that of Henry James and George Eliot, both of whom Miller discusses at length.

From here we see a connection to the sense of place that Southern literature famously has owned (and which I argue elsewhere in this text that Lovecraft also uses). Traditionally realistic though not utterly so, Southern literature is a critical part of the literary spine of *True Detective*. Southern landscapes are haunted by people, events, and memories, both present and past.

Miller cites several important twentieth-century philosophers, among them Jacques Derrida, and as one would expect, Derrida's thoughts on history come into play:

> The metaphysical concept of history . . . is the concept of history as history of meaning . . . history of meaning occurring, developing, fulfilling itself. Linearly . . . in a straight or circular line . . . The metaphysical character of the concept of history is not only linked to linearity but to a whole system of implications (teleology, eschatology, relevant and interiorizing accumulation of meaning, a certain type of traditionality, a certain concept of continuity, truth, etc.). This [linearity] is therefore not an accidental predicate which one could get rid of by a local ablation, in a way, without a general displacement of the organization, without making the system itself work. (460 in Miller; originally from *Positions* [Paris: Les Editions de Minuit, 1972], 77)

Derrida lays out what the Play does to its readers, their understanding of reality, and all that is subsumed under the concept of "reality." Derrida is discussing "history," but as Miller notes, "The formal structure of a novel is usually conceived of as the gradual emergence of its meaning. This coincides with its end, the fulfillment of the teleology of the work" (460). The Play replaces our usual notions of narrative with its own ahistorical, atemporal aesthetic, its own epistemology, ontology, and teleology. For those who encounter the Yellow King in Chambers, conventional notions of eschatology—death, judgment by a divine figure, reward and punishment, or simply endings—are replaced with insanity, isolation, and entrapment. Ends are as atemporal for Carcosa as they are in conventional modes, interestingly. No teleology is possible once the text of the Play falls into human hands. All teleology ends, changes, reverses; eschatology becomes an eternal trap without the possibility of redemption. It is a mockery of Christian hopes.

This has immediate implications for both Lovecraft and *True Detective*. In both, the "concept of . . . history as meaning" gets torn apart by powerful figures and cosmic horror. The notion of history "occurring, developing, fulfilling itself" becomes laughable when human participation in history is shown to be a parody of itself. Furthermore, Cohle's now-famous discourse on time, mimetically represented visually and verbally as the "time is a flat circle" flattened beer can statement, vis-à-vis Derrida becomes a mockery of conventional notions of history and historicity. Both Lovecraft and *True Detective* depend on Derrida's "whole system of implications" to provide the backdrop that cosmic horror destroys. The Yellow King in *True Detective* and cosmic horror in Lovecraft are the forces that generate the "general displacement" of history as a metaphysical concept.

The Play, both in Chambers and in those writers who have followed him, shows that the "somewhere" of our reality, the perceived ground of being whence we all act, is indeed a mask concealing the true reality of Carcosa. Similarly, the social reality in southern Louisiana, however warped and frequently corrupt, is still a mask for the characters in *True Detective*. Cohle's intellectualism distances him from the emotional reality of others, while Hart's philandering robs him of his family. Both men have to turn away from those coping strategies—put down their masks—and stand before the enormity of the cult of the Yellow King. The difficulty for those characters is that their masks are first necessary, then crippling. The masks Cohle and Hart wear have to be set aside before they can solve the mystery of the murders.

In *True Detective* and in Chambers, metonymy and metonymic transfer[6] occur through having the physical locations—southern Louisiana and Paris/ America, respectively—as the ground of meaning. From that ground and its associated roots in Southern Gothic (and ultimately back to both Faulkner and Poe), meaning changes from a direct, one-to-one association into a layered, contextual, complex system of meanings. There is no one, single meaning for anything in these works; instead, the reader must sift through layers of historical association, context, and culture, which are all altered by time, reader, and history. As deconstruction helps us to understand, this complexity and layering bridge narrative to its strategies, deceits, and implications. Burleson provides us with a concise summary of how deconstruction approaches these levels of understanding:

---

6. Metonymy occurs when one calls a thing or a concept not by its own name, but instead by the name of a thing or concept closely associated with it. Example: "The Pentagon" for the U.S. military.

> Some people have felt that [deconstruction's views] suggest that texts either mean nothing at all or can be made to mean anything (which would be tantamount to meaning nothing). Both suggestions derive from misconceptions. To begin with, texts end up meaning more than we might have thought, not less, when we submit them to the close readings that post-structuralism champions. We do not empty texts of their meaning; we deny only the privilege of univocal meanings to which texts might have been reduced. . . . [P]ost-structuralism recognizes and highlights the fact that the manner of functioning of texts within language is problematic. Texts tend to unravel themselves, tend to subvert their own apparently "ruling" logic. It is the purpose of deconstructive reading to discover how this self-subversion comes about. In pursuing the matter, we are not carping at the text for failing to have a consistency or integrity that it could have had. We are, on the contrary, showing that the text has the figural richness to partake fully of language. We are throwing light upon textual features that more simplistic readings would allow to remain hidden. (7)

Narrative is often haunted by its deceits, yet here Burleson shows us that what might seem to be meaningless, subversive play is in fact a reinforcement of the meaning and value of a given text. These layered, contextual systems of meanings become especially important in detective fiction in general and in *True Detective* in particular, as I discuss later in this work.

This construct of associations is stable insofar as no one seriously questions it or offers a different construct, but Carcosa in both Chambers and *True Detective* becomes that alternative construct. Metonymic transfer becomes impossible once someone reads the Play, because the power of the text, channeling the power of the Yellow King and Carcosa, pulls aside the mask, revealing the mask's existence and, more importantly, showing the haunted area inside.

For Lovecraft, the emphasis on realism means an emphasis, at least initially, on history and its accompanying narrative elements and processes. As Miller notes, "The notions of narrative, of character, and of formal unity in fiction are all congruent with the system of concepts making up the Western idea of history" (461). Lovecraft takes these assumptions and turns them inside out. Chambers takes them and turns them on humanity through the text of the Play. *True Detective* depends on them to provide a foil for the horrors of the cult of the Yellow King. As Miller observes, "'the historic mask' . . . the narrating of an historical sequence in one way or another involves a constructive, interpretative, fictive act" (461). There can be no fiction without some kind of mask, some gambit used by the author to present the work of fiction. For Miller, fiction is a gambit, first and foremost, a linguistic play used to establish common ground among those attempting communication.

A similar dynamic is involved with the Play. The Play rewrites history and reveals the mask that is not a mask; the Play subverts human sanity, thereby rendering history, interpretation, and the norms of narrative into its own "fictive act." Because the Play overwrites reality and the contents of the human mind, questions of history and personal narrative—"one's own story"—are no longer stable and reliable. For Miller, and Chambers before him, "narrative form becomes also obliquely a putting in question of history or of the writing of history" (462). Lovecraft's stories are fragments, incomplete histories, and, as referenced by Detwiller in *Delta Green,* impossible landscapes.[7] Weird fiction of Lovecraft's type destabilizes history, while that of The Play renders it useless. It is not just meaningless; it is useless.

Miller and other deconstructionists assure us that "Insofar as a novel 'deconstructs' the assumptions of 'realism' in fiction, it also turns out to 'deconstruct' naïve notions about history or about the writing of history" (462). The Play deconstructs human reality, showing it to be an impossibility. This is the whole point of the Yellow stories in Chambers's book: the wearing away of human reality as it is gradually, inevitably replaced with the reality of Carcosa and the realm of the Yellow King. It is both a demythologizing and a remythologizing, a dissolving of one set of histories, myths, and facts to make way for its replacement, as Miller's observations similarly note (467). *True Detective* uses the cult of the Yellow King to dismantle the metaphysics of history. It exposes metaphysics as a sham. All philosophical branches are a sham because human reality is a lie. The mores we believe make society function are simply a distraction that keeps the majority of people occupied while the followers of the Yellow King are free to act with little, and sometimes no, constraint. As Rust tells Marty in S1E7 "After You're Gone," "I think our man had a real good time after the hurricane."[8] In Chambers, Lovecraft, and *True Detective,* the demythologiz-

---

7. An attempt to examine the genre of Lovecraftian RPGs in any comprehensive way would be a book in itself.

8. "The hurricane" would be Katrina, which hit southern Louisiana in late August 2005 but concluded its path in Canada. Hurricanes carry a mythology of their own.

ing of history is in fact a remythologizing by using a different mythical base. It is a mythology that replaces hope with horror and ascension with insanity.

Miller tells us that "the writing of history [is] an act of repetition in which the present takes possession of the past and liberates it for a present purpose, thereby exploding the continuum of history" (471). Both Lovecraft and *True Detective* use the Play as a tool for this. For the followers of the Yellow King, Carcosa as a concept, if not an actual place, liberates them from the past and reshapes the present by creating a cul-de-sac of social and historical agency within which they can act with near perfect freedom and even license, thereby reshaping the future from being a mere repetition of present forms into an environment of near-absolute power and agency.

Nothing is spared in Lovecraft: no end, no origin, no way of knowing, no state of being. But from here, we can move toward *The King in Yellow* and examine how it seizes history, teleology, ontology, and epistemology.

Chapter 2: The Tatters of *The King*

THE GREEN ROOM

The Clown turned his powdered face to the mirror.

"If to be fair is to be beautiful," he said, "who can compare with me in my white mask?"

"Who can compare with him in his white mask?" I asked of Death beside me.

"Who can compare with me?" said Death, "for I am paler still."

"You are very beautiful," sighed the Clown, turning his powdered face from the mirror.

—Robert W. Chambers, *The King in Yellow*

Let your feelings slip, boy,
But never your mask, boy . . .
—Underworld, "Born Slippy"

Robert W. Chambers is best known today for his weird fiction, and for purposes here his book *The King in Yellow*,[1] but during his lifetime he made his fortune writing what were called "shop-girl romances" (Hite 186), immensely popular stories and novels about earnest, attractive, working-class girls who catch the eyes of rakes and who are able to redeem the young men from their risky, errant ways.[2] Even though some may point to these kinds of plots to give credence to the separation of art and commerce (see, for example, Jean-Jacques Rousseau's work *Discourse on the Origins of Inequality*), Chambers himself had no problem with commerce, saying, "I write what it pleases me to write; by luck it

---

1. Many thanks to M. Grant Kellermeyer for supplying a method of distinguishing among Chambers's works and ideas, which I discuss in the preface to this work. In addition, I use the phrase "the Yellow stories" and variants thereof to describe the sequence of stories in the Book that concern the Yellow King and the Play.

2. The Romance Writers of America list the following subgenres for romance novels published today: contemporary, erotic, historical, paranormal, romance with spiritual elements, romantic suspense, and young adult. Shop-girl romances probably fall into the latter.

may please the public" (Hite 186). For many authors such an attempt at artistic purity is contrived; sales figures and royalty checks are difficult if not impossible to ignore, and a string of shop-girl romances doesn't spring innocently from the pen. Nevertheless, Chambers's efforts were rewarded by publishers, the public, and publishing society, his prosperity only affected later by Prohibition and changing mores (Hite 186).

Chambers's influence on weird fiction is beyond debate. In his essay "Supernatural Horror in Literature" (1925–27), Lovecraft cites Chambers as a seminal influence on weird fiction in general (*CE* 2.109) and his own work in particular, lamenting Chambers's turn to popular fiction as a loss for the genre. Later authors who have been influenced by Chambers's work include James Blish, Joseph S. Pulver, Sr., Dennis Detwiller, Robin Laws, and many others. In both topic and style, Chambers's influence persists to this day, a matter I will cover later in this chapter.

How does one approach Chambers? The Book has sections that are straight short stories, but it also has a section of vignettes and prose poems in "The Prophets' Paradise" and a possible time-travel/alternative reality story in "The Demoiselle d'Ys." Establishing a timeline for the stories in the Book can be tricky: there are dates, places, and character names available, but they are neither thorough nor complete, and although multiple critics have tried to order Chambers's Yellow universe, the best efforts still end up as inconclusive.

This is perhaps the first message to carry with oneself when approaching Chambers. The details of the characters' times and environments are less important than the emotional timbre the characters carry within themselves. Their emotional lives are vibrant, if sometimes difficult (and for some, impossible to survive once the Yellow King approaches), and that vibrancy changes radically should they encounter and read the Play. In Chambers's early work, the characters' emotional lives are structured around close relationships—which is the case for humans in general—and an encounter with the Play is preceded by some key encounter that carries an emotional charge. This inciting incident renders the reader of the Play vulnerable to its effects.

It is too easy to write off the Book as just another part of the Decadent movement. These inciting incidents are the characters' first brushes with cosmicism, filtered through aesthetics and emotion. Chambers is influenced by the Decadents, to be sure (see, for instance, Kellermeyer's "Surreally Decadent" and Manchin's *Weird Britain*), but he is not bound by them. For these characters, the first brush with the realm of the Yellow King is catastrophic beyond the dilettantism of the Decadents.

The Book was Chambers's second and, to many, his most masterful publication. It is a collection of stories and prose poems, beginning with the poem "Cassilda's Song," a direct introduction to the ideas of there being a play, a place called Carcosa, a king in tattered robes, a lake, black stars, the Hyades, cloud waves, twin suns, death, and strange moons. These things are not utterly alien, but they nevertheless are both different and amplified at the same time. In 17 lines—16 lines of poetry plus the notation "Cassilda's Song in "The King in Yellow," Act i, Scene 2"—Chambers outlines the realm of Carcosa and its oddities.

In addition to "Cassilda's Song," the Yellow stories comprise

- "The Repairer of Reputations," an extended narrative from the point of view of Hildred Castaigne, who believes his cousin Louis to be the rightful heir to the throne of America and who covets the throne for himself. Here we find some of the most dramatic imagery of the Yellow King, including crowns, vestments, and the Yellow Sign itself; arguably, the Play's appearance here is a powerful incursion of Carcosa into our reality and marks, at least for Castaigne, an alternative history in which he finds himself living.[3]

- "The Mask," a story involving a quiescent lovers' triangle among artists in New York who encounter the Play but who find a degree of redemption through the death of one of them. Sculptor Boris Yvain concocts a potion that turns flesh into stone. Geneviève, Boris's beloved, becomes ill and reveals that she truly loves Alec (the narrator). Boris dies, and Alec becomes gravely ill, then recovers only to discover Geneviève is now turned into stone. Some time passes, then suddenly Geneviève returns to life (as do several small animals used as experiments by Boris).

- "In the Court of the Dragon," where the narrator has already read the Play and is drawn to follow an organist whose playing in church annoys the narrator's sense of aesthetics, then who in turn becomes a

---

3. Kellermeyer insists in multiple places in his edition of *The King in Yellow* that Castaigne's world is a hallucination. I find it instead to be a nearly full-bore incursion of Carcosa into Castaigne's mind, if not his world. As Chambers tells us, there are those who invite Carcosa and the Yellow King into our world.

sort of persecutor of the narrator.

- "The Yellow Sign," the crowning story of the Yellow stories and second only to "The Repairer of Reputations" in its demonstration of the power and effects of the Play. Here, an artist and his model first see a cemetery warden who seems to be stalking them, then they read the Play—the model reads it to tease the artist, then he reads it so that he does not lose her to it—and are lost to Carcosa and the Yellow King.
- "The Demoiselle d'Ys," an homage of sorts to Ambrose Bierce's story "An Inhabitant of Carcosa." Here, the narrator seems either to travel back in time or to enter an alternative dimension, where he encounters a young noblewoman and her court before once again finding himself in his own time.
- "The Prophets' Paradise," an homage to the *Rubaiyat* of Omar Khayyam (Hite 88n4; Kellermeyer King 112) and a series of prose poems that muse on such topics as death, beauty, love, deception, and fate. Each prose poem is lovely in itself, but Chambers only gestures at the topic, imagery, and meaning in each one, as if to use gesture drawing to address them—rather than completed images, they are quick, simplified sketches capturing the motion and essence rather than conveying the full appearance.

The last four stories—"The Street of the Four Winds," "The Street of the First Shell," "The Street of Our Lady of the Fields," and "Rue Barrée"—concern themselves with representational, realistic narratives about young, usually well-to-do male inhabitants of Paris and the various women they come to know, mostly in the context of the Franco-Prussian War of 1870–71. In many ways, these men and women are the most carnal of the characters in the Book, even though none of the elements associated with the Play or the Yellow King appear. They are decadent people without being lost to decadence.

Yet Chambers is not concerned with mere Decadence or realism; instead, he introduces cosmicism by expanding the moral listlessness of the Decadents into an all-encompassing, inescapable, total change from energy and ambition to distraction and abandonment. The Play doesn't challenge American values so much as it drains them away. The Yellow King and the promise of Carcosa push Chambers's characters into an outsideness that will later be matched in Lovecraft's narrators and investigators. Encounters with the Play lead to upset, violence, and even death. As Kenneth Hite notes in his annotations to *The King in Yellow,* "Discord remains a sign of the King's approach" (58n16).

As far as can be discerned from the Book, there seem to be only two acts in the Play. For the narrators of Chambers's Yellow stories, their encounters with Carcosa and the Yellow King have three parts: an initial act or event that seems innocent enough, then a critical encounter with the Play, and finally some evidence of Carcosa's incursion. The Play shows up at moments of crisis, as if to capitalize on the emotional vulnerability that crisis can bring about. As such, Chambers's Yellow stories become variations on the Edenic fall from grace. Castaigne, for instance, is an arch-deceiver, except he is self-deceived, attempting to destroy his cousin Louis's relationship with Louis's beloved, Constance. Alec, the narrator of "The Mask," is in love with Geneviève, the girlfriend of Boris Yvain, Alec's close friend and fellow artist. This unrequited love ultimately unbalances the silent love triangle Alec, Boris, and Geneviève have maintained, bringing about the death of Boris and a mystical redemption of Geneviève. The narrator of "In the Court of the Dragon" is self-deceiving about his powers of observation concerning the man who seems to be doubling or mirroring him, in a nod to multiple Poe stories. Finally, in "The Yellow Sign," the narrator Scott (who may or may not be the Jack Scott of "The Mask") knows he lacks the integrity needed to make a good mate for Tessie, his model (who may or may not also work as a prostitute), and indeed to make anyone a suitable husband. Scott's uncertainty and Tessie's weakness of character lead to their deaths after they read the Play. In the Yellow stories, everyone is damaged, and during their respective crises they turn to the Play and are corrupted by it.

This corruption is reflected in various ways in the cities in which Chambers's Yellow stories are set: New York and Paris, variously during the Belle Epoque and the 1920s.[4] Perhaps the most brutal evidence of the corruption of the times is the presence of the suicide chambers, first seen in "The Repairer of Reputations." Although some critics conclude that the chambers are a figment of Castaigne's imagination (Kellermeyer and Hite, among others), even those readers in favor of assisted suicide may pause at the effortlessness these machines offer. From the

---

4. Kellermeyer argues for Castaigne's insanity and delusion in "The Repairer of Reputations." Other authors (Robin Laws, for example) have taken Castaigne's world as reality, i.e., as evidence of incursions by Carcosa, and have teased out fascinating stories as a result.

point of view of this study, however, there is a striking parallel between the raw, unflinching reality of the suicide chambers and Thomas Ligotti's discussion of the locked room of the mind, a topic discussed in greater detail in chapter 3. Briefly, and as Ligotti would have it, the human mind, with its profound isolation not only from other people but also from reality itself, is little better than a suicide chamber with a victim waiting patiently within. Human life is impossible to tolerate because of the illusions surrounding human consciousness: the illusion of consciousness itself, the unreliability of the human body and its senses, the futility of human existence in the face of death. From this perspective, it is an easy walk to Rustin Cohle's "locked room" discourse in *True Detective* (S1E3).

Although Cohle's argument owes much to John Locke's analogy of the man in the locked room (see Locke's *An Essay concerning Human Understanding*, where he examines the idea of free will and its relationship to volition), Cohle's take on it is filtered through Ligotti, especially Ligotti's conception of humans as puppets, animated figures, and walking haunted houses.[5] Nevertheless, a philosophical error both Cohle and Ligotti make is to blur the distinction between a locked room and an internal life. Ligotti seems to dismiss the entire value of one's inner life, if not dismissing its existence outright. Cohle begins *True Detective* in 1995 as a damaged man, locked inside himself to keep himself from falling apart after the death of his daughter. His success with this psychological strategy turns his locked room into his own prison, where he remains isolated until the murders come to light, the cult's ongoing presence is revealed, and his investigation forces him to re-enter the world to confront Errol Childers. All this is possible—Ligotti, Cohle, *True Detective*—because of Lovecraft's admiration for Chambers, which later influences Ligotti's writings and worldview. Without Lovecraft, the bridge between Chambers and *True Detective* would be impossible to construct. Chambers influenced Lovecraft, who influenced Ligotti, who influenced Nic Pizzolatto, the creator of *True Detective*. Lovecraft is the keystone, even though Chambers and Ligotti get the attention.

Before the full discussion of *True Detective* begins in chapter 4, it will be necessary to outline and bring some shape to other ways the Book has appeared in popular culture. These form an important context for and a significant link between Chambers and *True Detective*. One of the key elements of the Book is how numerous characters have a highly developed sense of aesthetics—including those

---

5. I discuss this concept extensively in Chapter 3.

who are not artists—and how this sense of aesthetics affects their worldviews. For Chambers, as for Lovecraft after him and at times Poe before him, aesthetes and artists are more sensitive to changes in their environments than the average person, especially those changes that become corrupting influences.

The Decadent period, which took place during Chambers's adulthood,[6] had an immediate influence on him (even though he ultimately rejected it in favor of more lighthearted material; see Kellermeyer's analysis in his introduction to *The King in Yellow* 8–9). We see decadence as pervasive and almost invasive in characters such as Scott in "The Yellow Sign," whose sense of aesthetics renders him vulnerable to the physical text of the Play (Chambers, *Yellow Sign* 52). This vulnerability to the Play is axiomatic for those characters created by later writers adding to the Book's universe.

An important collection of stories related to Chambers is Joseph S. Pulver, Sr.'s *King in Yellow Tales, Volume 1*. Published individually between 1999 and 2012, the short pieces in this collection tease out the implications of Chambers's work in a modern setting, with modern characters reacting to the incursions of the Yellow King and Carcosa. The Yellow King walks, though barely perceptibly, among mankind in Pulver's universe, driving some to gleeful murder sprees, others to revenge, others to suicide, still others to madness. The "Carl Lee & Cassilda" trilogy (Pulver 15–52) presents characters with precedents in other stories, especially Karl Edward Wagner's "The River of Night's Dreaming." Wagner's story is a brilliant extension of weird fiction in general and Chambers's work in particular, combining an unreliable narrator who is a criminal, insane, or both, with a story that mines domestic fiction for its descent into the weird. The Play becomes the armature around which Wagner's main character's escape from confinement becomes another imprisonment. As we learn at the story's conclusion, the narrator of "The River of Night's Dreaming" had been at the mercy of the Yellow King during her imprisonment via the actions of a Dr. Archer (also a character in Pulver's collection, named after Hildred Castaigne's psychiatrist in "The Repairer of Reputations" and a character whom Castaigne may or may not have murdered). In Wagner's story, a copy of the Play is found among the main character's scant possessions. This interweaving of elements and narra-

---

6. The Decadent era in the United Kingdom grew out of, among other schools of thought, Victorian aestheticism and was most active during the late 19th century, though the movement in Italy it was of a much longer duration.

tive threads is characteristic of the texts that develop from the Book, as we will see later in the discussion of *True Detective* in chapter 4.

The aesthetic of Chambers's stories extends into other genres, especially that of tabletop role-playing games (RPGs). For instance, Chaosium, publishers of the award-winning game *Call of Cthulhu*, produced two notable long-term campaigns using Chambers's *The King in Yellow*: *Tatters of the King*, published in 2006, and *Ripples from Carcosa*, published in 2014.[7] Both campaigns detail the existence of cultists seeking Hastur, Carcosa, and the Yellow King in their desire to manifest Carcosa on Earth, with the Yellow King on the throne and Hastur reigning as the deity of Earth. Drawing on not only Chambers but also later authors such as James Blish and his critically important story "More Light," the campaign offers player characters (PCs) a chance to pursue cultists and prevent the ascendancy of Hastur and the Yellow King. Because of the association of Hastur and the Yellow King with the star Aldebaran, which becomes visible on Earth at regular intervals, the PCs and the characters they encounter in-game can never be fully safe, given Aldebaran's inevitable reappearance. Because humanity cannot escape these cycles, insanity and destruction are not only present with mankind; they are inevitable.

Another RPG using elements from Chambers is *Delta Green*, the most recent edition of which (published during 2020–21) was funded by a highly successful Kickstarter campaign that in turn spawned a number of supplemental texts as rewards for campaign supporters.[8] One of these supplements, *Impossible Landscapes*, comes as close as any text can to capturing the miasma generated by the Play. As a game setting, *Delta Green* is akin to *The X-Files*, the popular television show from the 1990s, in that *Delta Green* players take on the roles of quasi-government agents tasked with suppressing, destroying, or obstructing the manifestations of cosmic horror. *Impossible Landscapes* deals specifically with the play *The King in Yellow* and the havoc it wreaks across both centuries and planes of existence.

Unlike many systems where agents can become almost heroic as a conse-

---

[7]. There are numerous Chaosium publications to be examined; a considered discussion would be a book in itself, even if one disregarded the game supplements and related items published in secondary markets.

[8]. Originally published by Pagan Publishing, *Delta Green* is now published by Arc Dream Publishing.

quence of their battles with cosmic horror, the agents in *Impossible Landscapes* find themselves losing their understanding of reality and their hold on sanity until, by the end of the campaign, they realize that only Carcosa and the King in Yellow are real. Everything else has always been an illusion. There is no reality; there is no subjectivity. There never was. The only thing left is The King in his pallid mask, generating illusions in order to entrap humanity in a mind-bending world of ethereal uncertainty. Humanity's innate, inherent curiosity only strengthens the King's hold on those in his service and enables the King to entrap more followers. Carcosa's enveloping miasma can be postponed, but not defeated.

Above all else, *Impossible Landscapes* tells the tale of landscape shifting and changing as the agents move through it until it becomes nearly unrecognizable. This sense of change and lack of stability in a landscape point directly to another area of this study, the book *Petrochemical America,* which has immediate connections to the world of *True Detective*. Documenting the effects of a section of the petrochemical industry in a section of the Mississippi River colloquially known as "Cancer Alley," *Petrochemical America* examines the political, social, economic, and environmental effects of the industry on the land, people, and state. The consequences for the land and the people are profound: the industry wounds the land and water with persistent carcinogens, which are then transmitted into wildlife and people. Land values plummet as the coffers of the corporation swell, sending those not already sickened into desperate attempts to gain employment outside of their economically devastated communities. This wounding of the environment works its way up the social chain, corrupting residents, politicians, and people of all socioeconomic levels through their dependency on an economic base that destroys itself from within. As with addiction and other forms of dependence, the municipalities in Cancer Alley cannot rid themselves of the perpetrators and yet cannot survive without them.

This wounded landscape that can neither die nor survive, caught between life and death, is the landscape of both Chambers's victims and the characters in season 1 of *True Detective*. In Chambers, the Play changes the lives of the characters who read it through changing their understanding of the nature of the world. What was once the world most people agreed upon as reality now changes into an existence with Carcosa and the King lurking in the shadows, ever reminding the characters that they bear the mark of the King inside their psyches. There is no redemption for the world or for the characters. As in the game *Delta Green,* the landscape has become impossible. The violations of the landscape perpetrated by the Play and embodied by the mental illness that overcomes the characters in Chambers, in the game, and in *True Detective* is prefigured by Lovecraft's use of cosmic horror as a trope of woundedness, itself a trope used to describe the state of the enlightened ones within the unenlightened masses. Because certain sensitives such as artists have a deeper understanding of the weird, they serve as ambassadors of cosmic horror. This deeper understanding has a deleterious effect on them, driving them to extreme actions. Lovecraft uses woundedness to describe the plight of those who encounter cosmic horror in stories such as "The Unnamable" (1923), *At the Mountains of Madness* (1931), "The Dreams in the Witch House" (1932), and any number of other stories.

Yet another story collection influenced by Chambers is Robin Laws's collection *New Tales of the Yellow Sign* (hereafter referred to as *New Tales*), with its follow-up novel *The Missing and the Lost* (hereafter referred to as *The Missing*). The Play is the primary background for the characters in *New Tales* and is a part of the cultural context in both *New Tales* and *The Missing*. Far from being banned and copies being destroyed as in Chambers, *Delta Green,* and other stories, in *New Tales* the published, distributed Play has changed everything—the government, the laws, the rulers. Freedom has been replaced by constraint, trust by suspicion, democracy and representation by tyranny. The miasma of Carcosa has been embraced. Access to magic is present in both New *Tales* and *The Missing,* but it is controlled by shadowy figures (in the case of *The Missing*) and even by the text of the Play itself (e.g., as in the story "The Dog" in *New Tales*). In *The Missing,* even though the Castaigne dynasty has been overthrown (an act begun in "The Dog") and a feeble but strengthening democracy restored, those covertly aligned with the old regime and thus aligned with the Yellow King use magic to wage occult battles against the new order. Most characters in both books either don't know about magic or refuse to believe it is real, which is yet another triumph for those who follow the Yellow King. Being able to understand that this is happening in any capacity is an epistemological achievement for the characters in *The Missing*.

A similar miasmic effect can be found in the *Delta Green* world. In *Impossible Landscapes,* the experiences of the agents render it impossible for them to know the world as they once did. The Yellow Sign, the text of the Play, and eventually their adventures in Carcosa itself—necessary for the agents to complete if they are to find their own reality again—all replace what the agents once knew as reality. The Yellow Sign becomes a marker for withering sanity; the text of *The King in Yellow* overwrites all text it touches. The Play literally becomes all that can be read, learned, and understood. If the agents of Carcosa are successful, if the agents cannot complete their missions, the Play will become the only epistemic system available. The effect of the Play in *The Missing* is similar: a violent coup and a subsequent war were required to remove the Play's influence and the Yellow King's agents from the American government. Nevertheless, and in true weird fiction fashion, hidden agents remain, seeking to restore the Castaigne dynasty and, behind it, Carcosa.

The effect of the text of the Play in these other genres derives from Chambers, especially from his story "The Mask," where the narrator Alec has his thoughts overwritten by his reading of the Play. The truth does not rest after a confession from his beloved Geneviève; instead, beneath it, the Yellow King lurks and reveals himself during Alec's fevered state (Chambers, *Yellow Sign* 40–41). The Play opens the door for the entry of the Yellow King.

A similar experience happens to the narrator Mr. Scott (as noted by numerous critics and editors, he is possibly the same Jack Scott from "The Mask") in Chambers's story "The Yellow Sign." Once Scott and his model/girlfriend Tessie read the Play, they are permanently changed, so much so that the mushy-faced watchman they had both observed now attacks them, killing Tessie and mortally wounding Scott. Even though Scott avenges Tessie by killing the watchman, Scott cannot release his connection to Carcosa and the Yellow King; his soul seems to be eternally linked to the king despite the absolution he receives from a clergyman just before his death. By the end, Scott only comprehends reality through Carcosa and the Yellow King. This new epistemology, this new heuristic, has replaced his previous understanding of the world. Humanity's systems of power have been pushed aside and revealed to be puppets used by the Yellow King. The only reality is that of Carcosa.

With all this context in mind, a quick review of some of the key ideas in the Yellow stories is in order. In "The Repairer of Reputations," Chambers establishes cosmic horror without naming it as such. Castaigne feels the same kind of terrified attraction to the Play that Lovecraft's narrators feel as they investigate the weird and the strange:

> I started up and flung the book into the fireplace; the volume struck the barred gate and fell open on the hearth in the firelight. If I had not caught a glimpse of the opening words in the second act I should never have finished it, but as I stooped to pick it up, my eyes became riveted to the open page, and with a cry of terror, or perhaps it was of joy so poignant that I suffered I every nerve, I snatched the thing out of the coals and crept shaking to my bedroom, where I read it and reread it, and wept and laughed and trembled with a horror which at times assails me yet. This is the thing that troubles me, for I cannot forget Carcosa where black stars hang in the heavens; where the shadows of men's thoughts lengthen in the afternoon, when the twin suns sink into the lake of Hali; and my mind will bear forever the memory of the Pallid Mask. I pray God will curse the writer, as the writer has cursed the world with this beautiful, stupendous creation, terrible in its simplicity, irresistible in its truth—a world which now trembles before the King in Yellow. (Chambers, *Yellow Sign* 9)

Here we see one of the master tropes: mirroring. Through the act of exhibiting the words of the Play on the page, the Play turns the reader/viewer into an inhabitant of Carcosa. Enough turned inhabitants in a given city or country changes that place into Carcosa. Like the slow virus in William Gibson's *Neuromancer* or the virulent meme in Neal Stephenson's *Snow Crash*, the change is one of purity to contagion, a notion common among the Victorians and adapted for the present day. If we are all lapsarian, if there is no purity; if life is a perpetual fall from grace without redemption, then we are each of us in Carcosa already. The Play simply brings about the entry of the Yellow King. Castaigne tells someone—us? himself? a hallucination?—of its spread:

> It is well known how the book spread like an infectious disease, from city to city, from continent to continent. . . . No definite principles had been violated in those wicked pages, no doctrine promulgated, no convictions outraged. It could not be judged by any known standard, yet, although it was acknowledged that the supreme note of art had been struck in *The King in Yellow*, all felt that human nature could not bear the strain, nor thrive on words in which the essence of purest poison lurked. The very banality and innocence of the first act only allowed the blow to fall afterward with more awful effect. (Chambers, *Yellow Sign* 9)

The Play spreads like a meme, like slang, like a new and horrifying drug, like a new language and philosophy. It is a form of cosmic horror because it has no earthly precedent or parallel: it comes from outside, from unknown origins, with a power humans cannot resist. It overwhelms those with whom it comes into contact. As we see in Lovecraft, this is no simple brush with cosmic horror. It is absolute and totalizing. Kellermeyer notes, "So TKIY [Kellermeyer's abbreviation] does not proscribe immorality—it simply IS immorality, manifest and pure" (26). The purity of its immorality is an interesting idea, but for my purposes here the idea of the sign being replaced by the thing it represents and how that seems to provide full power and effect is more interesting. The Play would thus be an encounter with the noumenon, not the phenomenon. The Play is Art itself, presenting itself to mankind without the intercession of the artist or materials from which art may be created. Man stands before Art, exposed to the purity of the experience, and goes mad in response.

In addition to mirroring, other master tropes in the Book are masking, doubling, and woundedness. Masking/unmasking is key to Chambers's work *The King in Yellow*. Characters struggle with the social masks they are required to wear in light of the desires they feel for love, sex, and freedom, common enough for characters in fiction. More importantly, though, the mask functions as a locus and lever of power in the text. Who wears masks, who can and cannot remove his mask to reveal his true identity, and whose identity reveals vulnerabilities all become part of the revelation of control. Within this context, the Play puts masking and unmasking at the forefront, as quoted by Chambers in the chapter "The Mask":

> CAMILLA: You, sir, should unmask.
> STRANGER: Indeed?
> CASSILDA: Indeed, it's time. We all have laid aside disguise but you.
> STRANGER: I wear no mask.
> CAMILLA: (Terrified, aside to Cassilda.) No mask? No mask! (Chambers, *Yellow Sign* 33)

Once characters in the Book read the Play, they are socially unmasked, less able to fit within society's constraints. For instance, in the story "The Yellow King," we see Castaigne's vulnerability to the words of the play. Mere humans find the play irresistible even as they are cursed and destroyed through reading it. Although this bears obvious references to the Garden of Eden myth, there is something more subtle in Chambers's story. Castaigne masks his insanity in an effort to seize the "throne and the empire" of America (Chambers, *Yellow Sign*

32), which does not really exist (unless Castaigne is seeing the truth after his exposure to the Play, and Carcosa has begun an incursion). Alec masks his love for Geneviève to preserve his friendship with Boris, while the unnamed narrator of "In the Court of the Dragon" hides behind his mask of supposed superiority based on his skill at noticing fine details.

Other characters in Chambers, such as those in the vignettes in the chapter "The Prophets' Paradise," struggle with the way our masks obstruct us in our search to understand love, death, and beauty. For Chambers's characters, love and art are largely intertwined, and it is the heightened sensibilities of artists that make fuller access to love possible and that help them in their pursuits. At the same time, each chapter of Chambers's book is about loss in some way, and thus absence. All these are key elements of the detective's makeup in detective fiction, which I discuss in chapter 5.

Aesthetics is a critical element in the Book, and aesthetic sensibilities derived from artistic training form the basis of the characters' successes as quasi-investigators. Chambers's central characters—largely painters, but sometimes those involved in other arts, such as sculpture and theatre—have aesthetic sensibilities available only to those with training in the arts. Most of the chapters of the Book involve an encounter with beauty, such as the beauty of the Sylvia in "The Street of the First Shell" or Trent's encounter with war in the same story, or the beauty of the Sylvia of "The Street of the Four Winds," who is only a memory to the narrator Severn. It is through beauty that the narrators discover love. Their sense of aesthetics leads them to investigate moments of intensified beauty, such as when Selby, the central male figure in the story "Rue Barrée" and an art student, becomes involved with a beautiful prostitute, and when Alec, the narrator of "The Mask" and an artist, learns of Boris's development of a mysterious ossifying liquid, with effects such that it seems to intensify the beauty of the creature or item so ossified.

Chambers's narrators would seem to be conventional figures, then, but for the presence of the Play. The curiosity and determination possessed by Chambers's narrators both moves them toward love and, in some instances, toward madness and death when that same curiosity and determination, along with the power of the very text of the play, lures them into the shadow realm of the Yellow King. It is these heightened artistic sensibilities that figure so strongly for both H. P. Lovecraft's narrators and Rustin Cohle in *True Detective*.

For Lovecraft, unlike Chambers, aesthetic sensibilities can lead beyond encounters with mere beauty to encounters with cosmic horror (Poirier, "Ripples" 10). There are numerous examples of this in Lovecraft. In the short novel *At the Mountains of Madness* (1931), Dyer, Danforth, and other members of the Antarctic search team learn the history of the Old Ones via the art left behind in their city. Without this historical record, Dyer would not have been able to conclude, "Radiates, vegetables, monstrosities, star-spawn—whatever they had been, they were men!" (*CF* 3.143). The end of these encounters, as with much of the rest of Lovecraft, is an encounter with a truth heretofore unknown and the mind-rending understanding of the glimpse of the reality behind our everyday reality.

These narrators in both Chambers and Lovecraft become investigators whether voluntarily or not, attracted to a set of circumstances often (but not always) by a desire to encounter aesthetically pleasing experiences. An example is "The Music of Erich Zann" (1921), where a passerby is attracted to violin music but encounters a window into the cosmic gulf when he investigates too far (*CF* 2.280–90). Aesthetics and investigation become linked, with the investigation's outcome depending on following clues, in some instances clues associated with art, and understanding the message behind the clues via artistic appreciation. This linkage between aesthetics and investigation becomes important for detective fiction, as I discuss in chapter 5.

Interestingly, aesthetics and epistemology—that is, the study of how we know what we know—also become linked by the principle and the act of investigation. To understand an aesthetic, we must also understand at least some of how we perceive and understand the work of art before us. (This need not be complex, but it certainly can be.) We need to be able to understand how we know what we know about our response, which is an act of epistemology. If we have an incomplete understanding of our encounter with a work of art, our understanding of ourselves in the work's presence is diminished yet perhaps piqued at the same time. This epistemological inquiry is itself an act of investigation, with the goal behind it being a more nuanced understanding of the aesthetic involved with the work of art. In some ways, we cannot easily appreciate a work of art without employing epistemology and investigation to adequately explore the aesthetics employed and referenced by the artist, in addition to grasping our own response to them.

The Play is both an aesthetic and an epistemology. It is an aesthetic because it lures the reader into its world by performing an irresistible act of intellectual seduction. The play traps readers through both language and ideas. In part III of "The Yellow Sign," the narrator Scott has fallen to the temptation of reading his copy, as has his model Tessie. After finishing it, they talk, though at first without realizing they spoke of the play (Chambers, *Yellow Sign* 52). They talk and talk of it because they can no longer talk of anything else. The play has replaced their former mindset with itself. And because, once read, the play dominates the mind of the reader, it becomes an epistemology, a hermeneutic, an aesthetic. It becomes the way the reader sees, knows, and understands the world. The Yellow King replaces others with himself, and Carcosa replaces our reality with itself.

Scott's despair at the beauty of the Play becomes a painful, crippling event, considering that he is an artist:

> Oh, the sin of writing such words—words which are clear as crystal, limpid and musical as bubbling springs, words which sparkle and glow like the poisoned diamonds of the Medicis! Oh, the wickedness, the hopeless damnation of a soul who could fascinate and paralyze human creatures with such words—words understood by the ignorant and wise alike, more soothing than music, more awful than death! (Chambers, *Yellow Sign* 67)

The new aesthetic sent by the Yellow King to humanity leaves Scott and Tessie "speaking for some time in a dull monotonous strain" and without realizing "the gathering shadows" (67). This is a new aesthetic of darkness, indirection, loss, and initiation into an order dominated by Carcosa and the Yellow King. Scott tells us, "Night fell and the hours dragged on, but still we murmured to each other of the King and the Pallid Mask. . . . We spoke of Hastur and Cassilda, while outside the fog rolled against the blank window-panes as the cloud waves roll and break on the shores of Hali" (67–68). The Play, once read, supplants desire with languor, work with distraction, art with decadence, imagination with images of Carcosa. There is no return from this new aesthetic. Carcosa destroys artists by replacing their intrinsic nature as artists with its own, more powerful, more totalizing manifestation of decadence. It is an initiation into terrible truths, as Scott discovers that "I knew that she knew and read my thoughts as I read hers, for we had understood the mystery of the Hyades and the Phantom of Truth was laid" (68). Here we see Scott's powers as an artist replaced by what seems to be telepathy, or at the very least a mode of nonverbal communication that brings minds parallel in terms of thought, so that communication seems to be taking place. But it is not the authentic communication of one's thoughts or emotions; instead, Carcosa and the King in Yellow have supplanted Scott and Tessie's inner lives. Their lives are now those of the inhabitants of Carcosa.

Near the end Scott tells us, "Then, as I fell, I heard Tessie's soft cry and her spirit fled; and even while falling I longed to follow her, for I knew that the King in Yellow had opened his tattered mantle and there was only God to cry to now" (68). Interestingly, the Yellow King's powers over humans are greater than those of the conventional Deity. In fact, the Yellow King leaves man without hope: "I would tell more, but I cannot see what help it will be to the world" (68). Here, perhaps, is the strongest statement Chambers makes about art and the artist. Instead of creating art for the sake of beauty, or ornament, or message, or communication with other artists, or for art's sake, or for public or private commission, the artist Scott gives up on trying to tell the rest of humanity what he now knows. Scott is changed into an artist without art, without skill or craft, without purpose, without an aesthetic. An artist without art has only death as a recourse, which seems to be Scott's ultimate fate.

Lovecraft notes the presence of Carcosa in the human psyche in his essay "Supernatural Horror in Literature" (1925–27): "some nightmare memory of [Carcosa] seems to lurk latent and ominous in the back of all men's minds" (Lovecraft, *Annotated* 69). More than the Freudian death wish, or the classical Greek linkage of Eros and Thanatos, or the Nietzschean will to power, somewhere among those Carcosa waits, brooding and dim under its black stars. It is an incursion of power into the place inhabited by the powerless.

Chapter 3: Thomas Ligotti and the Unreliability of Human Understanding

I was never *really* insane, except upon occasions where my heart was touched.
—Edgar Allan Poe, letter to Maria Clemm (7 July 1849)

Madness, mayhem, erotic vandalism, devastation of innumerable souls—while we scream and perish. History licks a finger and turns the page.
—Thomas Ligotti, *Songs of a Dead Dreamer*

Coming at Thomas Ligotti's *The Conspiracy against the Human Race* (hereafter *Conspiracy*) requires a complex orientation. Ligotti's philosophical treatise is nonfiction that deals with fiction and supposition via the lens of philosophical pessimism, generally through Arthur Schopenhauer's work but more specifically through the translated writings of Norwegian philosopher Peter Wessel Zapffe, who is as bleak a pessimist as anyone could want. Ligotti begins, as does Zapffe before him, with a scenario illustrating the awakening of human consciousness and the recognition by the new Homo sapiens that his consciousness is an evolutionary mistake. Ligotti teases out the ramifications of this mistake, insisting that, contrary to the opinion of most others, being alive is not all right and that the only honorable choice is suicide so that we may reject the alternatives of being the equivalent of either a zombie or a puppet. The human body is haunted by its consciousness, according to Ligotti (see, for example, *Conspiracy* 28) and thus is denied real dignity and agency.

By his own admission, Ligotti has been influenced by Lovecraft, an influence that scholars and critics have thoroughly reviewed (among others, Pollard; Woodard; Feltham; Trigg; Cardin; Joshi; Sheedy) and which I will not reproduce here. The difficulty Ligotti faces is twofold: one, distinguishing his approach to horror, and two, settling the roots of his horror in some kind of philosophical approach. In accordance with his own temperament, Ligotti approaches horror and life in general through philosophical pessimism. This chapter addresses Ligotti's pessimism as it relates to *True Detective* and, to a lesser extent, the works of H. P. Lovecraft and other pessimists as context.

Ligotti openly acknowledges his debt to Lovecraft (Cardin 96), though it is based on Ligotti's embrace of what he sees as Lovecraft's own worldview, more so than with ideas represented in Lovecraft's fiction. In *Conspiracy*, the overwhelming influence on Ligotti is Peter Wessel Zapffe, specifically Zapffe's 1933 essay "The Last Messiah." From the beginning of his essay, Zapffe maintains that human consciousness is a curse that makes us aware of the suffering of all life. He describes the awakening of human consciousness as "[a] breach in the very unity of life, a biological paradox, an abomination, an absurdity, an exaggeration of disastrous nature." Zapffe's sense of betrayal extends to all humanity, past and present, "a senseless squander of organic material." Zapffe acknowledges the existence of genetic mutations but insists they "must be considered blind, they work, are thrown forth, without any contact of interest with their environment." Suddenly awakened to higher consciousness at random, purposeless, without direction, man is crushed by this knowledge, with a tiny fraction of humanity taking what Zapffe and Ligotti see as the honorable way out—suicide—and the rest finding ways to distract themselves from their burden of consciousness.

For Zapffe, and for Ligotti in his footsteps, this is a matter of "artificially limiting the content of consciousness." Zapffe sees four ways that humans artificially limit their consciousness: isolation, anchoring, distraction, and sublimation (Ligotti in *Conspiracy* introduces the concepts at 31–32 and uses them as touchstones throughout the book). We find ways to remove thoughts about our doom: dismissing them to the back rooms of our minds; trusting in social structures like schools, jobs, and achievements; finding other things to do; and for some, creating art. For Zapffe and Ligotti, these limits are the real betrayal that humanity enacts on itself because they turn human attention away from its condition.

Yet these limits are necessary for most of us. With cognitive limitations in hand, we construct a personal narrative—the threads we pull together and claim as a life—as we seek to both escape from our core terror and strive toward something we label as "better," "higher," or that which has been otherwise set by our culture as an honorable and good end. Without means to repress our core terror, we cannot function, we cannot build and maintain society, and, as it seems at least for Ligotti, we cannot stop being a source of annoyance to pessimists, who are the fraction of humanity who refuse to look away from that core terror. For Ligotti and Zapffe, this personal narrative is nothing more than a lie that keeps us from facing the horror of consciousness. Fortunately, Zapffe sees a savior of sorts in a figure he calls the Last Messiah, a man who has faced and accepted the truth about human consciousness and death and who announces the true salvation of humanity: infertility. Appropriately enough, Zapffe believes that this messiah will be destroyed by humanity for daring to speak the truth (10). One may imagine Zapffe's satisfaction at this outcome.

Zapffe's essay is not without its problems. He begins it with a conjured image of the first man awakening to consciousness and ultimately refusing to live. (Interestingly, the man's wife does not share in awakened consciousness, and indeed, part IV of Zapffe's essay, if published today, would be culturally problematic to some modern scholars, even though it is consistent with ideas current in Zapffe's time.) Zapffe's awakened man is as alone as Nietzsche's superman, with the obvious yet unwritten extrapolation for the reader being the awakened man's superiority over the distracted masses.[1]

Both Zapffe's and Ligotti's ideas lead to some interesting questions. For instance, how was Zapffe influenced by World War I and its horrors? Zapffe's entire corpus has not been translated as of this writing, so answers may be locked within the Norwegian of his manuscripts. Both Ligotti and Zapffe in his translations insist that human consciousness amounts to betrayal or worse. Zapffe states that the awakened man has been "betrayed by the universe," yet Zapffe either will not or cannot account for agency or mechanism in this betrayal. What are the ways that betrayal is enacted? Betrayal is an action, after all; it is a decision first, then one or more steps taken. Zapffe notes genetic mutations but dismisses them, and he does not consider the effects of evolution and natural selection, which allow mutations to be passed on to future generations, provided the mutations give the organism an environmental advantage. Both Zapffe and Ligotti, Zapffe more so, seem to presume that any time a person sees through the various tricks he uses on himself and subsequently encounters the utter lack of meaning—the gap of nothingness between birth and death—the person will react with an overwhelming sense of "dread of being" or with the

---

1. Ligotti offers his own take on Nietzsche in *Conspiracy* (120–24 is the most intensive examination). From there, the connections to Zapffe are clear.

determination not to be out-argued (see, for example, Ligotti 64). Any other stance betrays one as an optimist, it would seem. Yet still one feels compelled to ask, what next? What happens when a person accepts the blunder? Is that all? Are our choices limited to cowardice or suicide?

For all his insistence, Ligotti runs into the same wall in *Conspiracy* again and again, chapter after chapter. Beyond simple existential meaninglessness, human life is a betrayal and a deceit, a betrayal from without (man's "awakening") and a deceit from within (man-as-puppet). For some contemporary readers, these ideas are not totally far-fetched. But once one accepts them as an accurate statement on epistemology and etiology, what then? Zapffe's and Ligotti's intransigence pushes them close to the "no true Scotsman" fallacy—no real optimist would be able to accept the depths of horror that Zapffe and Ligotti have experienced—yet still we may ask, what then? Both Ligotti and Zapffe are silent, and notably alive, in their respective eras. Neither Zapffe nor Ligotti have much to offer beyond their insistence and condemnation, yet the clock still ticks and time passes for those of us still living.

Another limitation in Ligotti's and Zapffe's respective arguments is their insistence on a limited range of ways to cope with one's recognition of human insignificance. Other writers have seen beyond this limited set of coping mechanisms, including prominent Lovecraft scholars. In a past issue of *Lovecraft Studies*, S. T. Joshi and K. Setiya present excerpts from their correspondence on Lovecraft, specifically, Lovecraft's take on cosmic horror and man's response to it. In the excerpts, Setiya essentially rejects the stance of both Ligotti and Zapffe:

> I don't think that scientists will ever be horrified by their discoveries, nor am I horrified that man is insignificant in cosmic terms—we are free to make our own values and our own ethics, and cosmicism has little or nothing to do with it; only atheism as a part of cosmicism is directly related to ethics. (23)

Joshi generally agrees:

> I think you are absolutely right that the fundamental point in Lovecraft is man's inability to accept scientific rationalism, not an inability to cope with it . . . . But I also think (and I've said this a number of times in print) that Lovecraft, being himself so much a creature of intellect, had an exaggerated sense of the power of the intellect to guide human affairs. The fact is that the majori-

ty of people in the world are not governed by their rational minds but by irrational habit or custom. (34)

This is the great weakness in Ligotti and Zapffe: their inability to accept scientific rationalism *as it extends to humans*—individual, lone humans—like themselves. In the broad sense, they speak of humans en masse, but their discussions of how humans lack the power to accept humanity's lot always turn to the individual and his inner life. Here, Ligotti and Zapffe inhabit the locked room of their own psyches, haunted by what they both find and do not find there. Outside that locked room, they do not accept that being able to cope with the cosmic horror of human insignificance is anything less than being optimistic (in Ligotti) or limiting one's consciousness (in Zapffe). No other options are possible.

Ligotti and Zapffe's positions depend on a hyper-rational participant. They are not only angry that the lot of humanity is to die, they are also annoyed that so few others are angry about it. This fury at reality is occasionally baffling and, I find, represents a limitation of imagination. If the individual is a puppet hallucinating a reality it cannot verify inside a brain it cannot trust, then what does the puppet care if other puppets are self-deceiving? Indeed, can the puppet be sure of their self-deceit? The centripetal force of Ligotti and Zapffe's ideas bind them both.

But why should Zapffe and Ligotti be correct about the base conditions of humanity? Zapffe's position we may possibly excuse because, born in 1899, he was in his adolescence during the horrors of World War I, no doubt a formative experience. Ligotti is post–World War II, with its even greater horrors, yet he is also part of the world and the Western culture that had to come to terms with those events. Other individuals faced those horrors and came through, horrors compounded by the fact of lurking human insignificance just beyond them. Many survivors, well aware of the insignificance of man, found a way through and a way back. Yet here we have Ligotti, waving all this away with Zapffe's four pillars of limited consciousness. The bottom for Ligotti, the darkest point, is mere insignificance.

Yet Ligotti keeps battling, even though his pessimism meets the fact of death, plops down, and begins to wail. Ligotti keeps trying to find a way for his brand of pessimism to move forward, but he runs into these dead ends time and again (e.g., the chapter "The Nightmare of Being," where Ligotti hits multiple dead ends and just stops at each one). He and the other pessimists are angry about suffering and death—and that's it. Zapffe is angry that human consciousness is not solely occupied with hardscrabble existence, like that of animals (so far as we know). Yet Ligotti concedes that Lovecraft, Schopenhauer, and Zapffe "pursued gratifying diversions that took their minds off what [Schopenhauer] called the 'vanity and suffering of life'" (*Conspiracy* 60–61). No doubt Ligotti does these things himself, a matter he hints at occasionally in the text, but in other places in *Conspiracy* Ligotti portrays pessimism as all-consuming. Which one is it? Ligotti seems to castigate mankind for being distracted by the made-up elements of its culture, which is to say, all human culture in all eras, yet Ligotti's pessimist forbears did the same without receiving a full measure of castigation from him.

Ultimately, one wonders if Ligotti, Zapffe, and others aren't taking death and uncertainty a little too personally. They take what they claim to be their awareness of man's insignificance and then draw from it, ironically, what appears to be a measure of self-inflation. If they really believed in man's insignificance, why would they feel affronted by death, by the limitations of human awareness, and by the man-puppet existence of the individual? It, too, means nothing. That affront may belie their actual feelings of the worth and value of human life and consciousness. If human consciousness and suffering are ultimately without meaning, if human death is without meaning, then where do human relationships have a place? Zapffe in his essay and Ligotti in *Conspiracy* do not examine relationships to any extent. As Pollard notes, this omission means Ligotti does not devote much discussion to ethics in *Conspiracy;* Ligotti waves off ethics as a "relatively soft cognitive pastime" (Pollard 139; Ligotti 72). Ligotti quotes Epicurus on death, but he never discusses why he himself cannot or will not adopt Epicurus's position:

> Whatever causes no annoyance when it is present, causes only a groundless pain in the expectation. Death, therefore, the most awful of evils, is nothing to us, seeing that, when we are, death is not come, and when death is come, we are not. (Ligotti discussing Epicurus, *Conspiracy* 157)

It is possible that Ligotti doesn't adopt it because Epicurus' position negates that of the pessimists. Human consciousness is itself not an "annoyance"; it is the awareness of death that makes consciousness a burden for Ligotti, Zapffe, and others. Yet here is Epicurus, pointing out that the burden is "groundless pain" because of expectation, not because of the burden itself. The groundless pain comes from a human act of decision making, not an external condition imposed on man. Ligotti makes no effort to counter this negation.

Oddly, Ligotti seems to express himself most directly not in the full analysis he presents in the body of *Conspiracy*, but in other places in the text: the first, quotations from "Professor Nobody" at the end of some chapters, where he quotes his own essay "Professor Nobody's Little Lectures on Supernatural Horror" from his book *Songs of a Dead Dreamer;* the second, in the few endnotes to the book, where Ligotti is more open and casual. The most telling thing in Ligotti, however, may be the third, the epigraph to *Conspiracy,* which is a translated passage from the *Dhammapada:*

> Look at your body—
> A painted puppet, a poor toy
> Of jointed parts ready to collapse,
> A diseased and suffering thing
> With a head full of false imaginings.

That is one translation of the Buddha's statement. Here is a slightly different one:

> Behold this body—a painted image, a mass of heaped up sores, infirm, full of hankering—of which nothing is lasting or stable! (Buddha Dharma)

Aside from being a prose translation rather than a verse translation, the second one emphasizes the experience of being in one's body rather than viewing it with detachment, the latter of which is Ligotti's perspective. Here is a third translation:

> For behold your body—
> A painted puppet, a toy,
> Jointed, sick and full of false imaginings,
> A shadow that shifts and fades. (Byrom)

The third translation lacks the emphasis on the core pessimistic philosophy of suffering, though suffering is certainly a Buddhist tenet. Instead, this translation emphasizes the transitory nature of things, another tenet of Buddhism. One thing Ligotti overlooks in his epigraph and treats only briefly in *Conspiracy* is the matter of choice.² The Buddha goes on to say in the same chapter from Byrom's translation of *The Dhammapada,*

> My mind has reached the Unconditioned:
> I have attained the destruction of cravings. (58)

In Ligotti's etiology, ontology, epistemology, and teleology, there is little room for spiritual choice or growth, much less the freedom that comes from enlightenment, because humans are puppets, lied to by their own senses and burdened with consciousness too great for the simple task of living, a burden that complexifies existence without providing any benefit.

For Ligotti, human consciousness is a monad, static and unchanging. Although this limitation to consciousness is central to the definition of pessimism as Ligotti presents it, it comes at the cost of bracketing off context. Unfortunately, there is a contextual and historical problem with Ligotti's insistence that we are "hunks of spoiling flesh on disintegrating bones" (28): the denial of the Will-to-Live in Schopenhauer is rooted in Indian mysticism, not anti-natalism, so Schopenhauer's denial is in fact akin to transcendence.³ But Ligotti doesn't even look at it: "While commentators on Schopenhauer's thought have seized upon it as a philosophical system ripe for academic analysis, they do not emphasize that its ideal end point—the denial of the Will-to-Live—is a construct for the end of human existence" (30). Although Ligotti's statement is consistent with his teleology—Ligotti is nothing if not consistent with that—the epigraph to his book is part of a larger testament from The Buddha that transcendence, not death, is the desired end for humanity. Ligotti sets an epigraph that apparently he doesn't fully believe in.

One of the knock-on errors this position introduces is what seems to be a confusion on Ligotti's part, or perhaps it is a conflation, of purposes and ends. Ligotti states flatly,

> Consciousness is an existential lullaby, as every pessimist agrees—a blunder of blind nature, according to Zapffe, that has taken humankind down a black hole

---

2. Ligotti devotes only six pages of *Conspiracy* to Buddhism (129–35), dismissing it as "a compilation of do-it-yourself projects."

3. As noted by Thompson in his article in *The Critique,* Schopenhauer relied on "early, inaccurate" translations of Hindu and Buddhist texts and thus offered misinterpretations through no fault of his own, making those spiritual traditions out to be more pessimistic than they are.

of logic. To make it through this life, we must make believe that we are not what we are—contradictory beings whose continuance only worsens our plight as mutants who embody the contorted logic of a paradox. (52)

The paradox as stated by Ligotti numerous times is that the purpose of life is death. However, the conflation here permits Ligotti to use both senses of τέλος: "end" and "purpose." The *end* of life is death; the *purpose* of life is a much broader idea and a much wider discussion. Even Schopenhauer's "philosophical superstructure" (54) with its Will-to-Live as motivator gets waved away by Ligotti, who states instead that the things activated by the Will-to-Live have no basis in reality because they are "only puppets" that "mistakenly believe they are self-winding persons who are making a go of it on their own" (54). If we are puppets, then of what use is the Will-to-Live? None, according to Ligotti.[4] Both Ligotti and Zapffe describe the Will-to-Live as a force, then wave it off. If this is so, one wonders why either of them went to the trouble to set down their thoughts.

Truly, the only authors who are provided with context in *Conspiracy* are the authors with whom Ligotti agrees (e.g., Bahnsen [13–14], Michelstaedter [32–33], Mainländer [34–38], Saltus, Unamuno, and Brashear [47–49], Nietzsche [passim][5]), and of course Schopenhauer throughout the text of *Conspiracy,* who, as arguably the best-known and most widely read pessimist, seems to get briefer treatment than he deserves from Ligotti. Zapffe above all others forms the basis of Ligotti's positions in *Conspiracy,* all from a 14-page essay published in 1933. In comparison, Lovecraft's pessimism derives from his materialism, and because Lovecraft's personal code meant he could neither drown his pessimism in drink nor plead with a given deity for rescue, he was left with writing weird fiction for relief (Joshi, *Evolution* 81).

Other writers have observed Ligotti's efforts through various lenses: Woodard, via philosophy, notes the differences between Ligotti and Lovecraft, including an excellent examination on Ligotti and his focus on "conditions of access and subjectivism at the expense of the real or nature" (7). Ligotti's philosophy in *Conspiracy* absolutely over-focuses on access, i.e., epistemology—

---

4. This dismissal enables both Ligotti and Zapffe to avoid treating the question of ethics with anything more than "suicide is the only honorable choice," as observed by John Pollard in his excellent critique.
5. Page numbers refer to *Conspiracy*.

how can we possibly trust what our unreliable senses tell us—at the expense of the real, which Ligotti vaguely dismisses, and nature, which does not participate in humanity's agonies. James Machin provides an excellent, condensed review of Kant and Schopenhauer before examining the latter's importance to Lovecraft's fiction vis-à-vis "The Music of Erich Zann" (1921), a story that Ligotti also examines (*Conspiracy* 193–94). Dylan Trigg discusses Lovecraft's vision of reality through "epistemic certainties concerning human access to the world" (3–4). For Trigg, Lovecraft's philosophical horror tells humans they aren't alone, aren't powerful, aren't unique, aren't the recipients of specialized knowledge, aren't informed about the true nature of the cosmos, aren't correct about their notions of reality, and aren't able to change any of this. Trigg notes the importance of Ligotti to this "atmosphere of philosophical horror" (3). Timothy Jarvis notes Ligotti's "Cosmic Pessimism" (12; capitalization in the original text) and that Lovecraft's use of degeneracy became "a strange cosmic perspective which made [it] a condition of the universe" (5). He also brings in Julia Kristeva's *Powers of Horror* and her work on abjection, especially as it involves the past (12), a concept that I address in chapter 6.

Ligotti's identification with Lovecraft as a fellow pessimist is well documented. He describes Lovecraft as "a paragon among literary figures who have thought the unthinkable, or at least thought what most mortals do not want to think" (57):

> *The Case of Charles Dexter Ward* is in every way a negation of [William Peter] Blatty's *Exorcist*. In Lovecraft's novel, the universe cares nothing for human life, just as it is in the real world, and one does not care about the characters—they are only a perspective from which to view the horror of the plot. (203)

Ligotti's point about some of Lovecraft's characters is well taken. Many of them do not have names, only vague physical bodies, and often they are unreliable. What they do have is a nearly insatiable curiosity[6] about strange events that eventually become matters of cosmic horror:

> Everyone, not only the hapless protagonist of the book, exists in a world that is a wall-to-wall nightmare. In Lovecraft's *universe without a formula*, everyone is killable—and some kill themselves just ahead of the worse things waiting for them . . . He simply wants to say that we no longer have to stand back very far

---

6. Matt Cardin in his excellent essay uses the term *sehnsucht* ("infinite longing that is the essence of romanticism"), an idea I address later in this chapter.

to see that the human race is what it always has been in this or any other world—irrelevant, which is as liberating to some as it is maddening to others, including Lovecraft's characters. (204; emphasis in the original text)

Unfortunately, Ligotti seems to return to the position that Lovecraft inhabited such a universe internally (204–5) and coped with pessimism by using strategies similar to the ones found in Zapffe. However, Lovecraft's letters do not universally present this kind of mindset in him.[7] Stretching poor Lovecraft to cover all this philosophical, emotional, and psychological ground almost becomes too much for the reader, and likely for Lovecraft, to accept.

Ligotti splits Lovecraft into the "perfectionist of cosmic disillusion" and the "one who reveled in protectionist illusions," calling the former Lovecraft's "alter ego" (Ligotti 60). Ligotti provides an exegesis of Lovecraft via Zapffe, noting Lovecraft's "anchorings" and distractions via his love of history, art, architecture, and New England in general (60). Paraphrasing Schopenhauer, Ligotti states that "Lovecraft was exhilarated by the idea of something pernicious that made a nightmare of our world, whether it was indifferent to us or quite partial to our devastation" (61). For Ligotti and Schopenhauer, that pernicious element is optimism; for Lovecraft, it is cosmic horror. Ligotti and Lovecraft come at this from two different ends, a matter carefully explored by Matt Cardin.

Cardin's treatment of Ligotti and Lovecraft looks at the evocation of mood, the use of realism, and the importance of aesthetics in these two authors. Cardin distinguishes a critical point of difference between them:

> Lovecraft . . . was emotionally and intellectually focused on the horror of "cosmic outsideness," of vast outer spaces and the mind-shattering powers and principles that may hold sway there, and that may occasionally impinge upon human reality and reveal its pathetic fragility. . . . Ligotti, by contrast, seems focused more upon the horror of deep *insideness*, of the dark, twisted, transcendent truths and mysteries that reside within consciousness itself and find their outward expressions in scenes and situations of warped perceptions and diseased metaphysics. (112–13; emphasis in original)

Cardin characterizes Lovecraft as "outer, transcendent, cosmic" and Ligotti as "inner, immanent, personal" (113). Lovecraft's detachment is the opposite of

---

7. One need only read Lovecraft's spontaneous poem on Charlie Chaplin (*Letters to Rheinhart Kleiner and Others* 41) to verify this.

Ligotti's enmeshment, despite other similarities the authors share, and this difference becomes part of the larger divergence between the two.

Considering Ligotti's exegesis of Lovecraft, Cardin's essay on the Ligotti-Lovecraft relationship is especially valuable. One of the notable items is Cardin's coverage of Ligotti's self-admitted psychological conditions: depression (95), anxiety-panic disorder (96), chronic anxiety (97), agoraphobia (98), and anhedonia (120).[8] One cannot help but wonder if these contribute to what would amount to an extreme sense of inwardness, a perspective that Cardin contrasts with Lovecraft's "outsideness" later in the essay (112–13).

In examining Ligotti versus Lovecraft as writers, Cardin looks at mood versus supernatural realism and Ligotti's emphasis on the importance of capturing a mood that is almost a physical sensation (12). Although Lovecraft's early stories masterfully captured mood, they were arguably less successful than his later stories, where realism became the context for cosmic horror. Ligotti's preferences for the early Lovecraft are consistent with a universe without a formula, given that a universe with a formula would be full of annoying optimists. Ligotti goes so far as to critique Albert Camus's take on the myth of Sisyphus, observing that "[Camus's] insistence that we *must* imagine Sisyphus as happy is as impractical as it is feculent" (40). In some ways, Sisyphus is the ultimate actor in a universe without a formula because there is only one formula—that of the rock and the hill. In that universe, there are no "vague, elusive, fragmentary impressions of wonder, beauty, and adventurous expectancy" that Lovecraft sought to write about (Cardin 120). Fortunately, Lovecraft's universe allowed for those impressions, and from them, we are ultimately led to cosmic horror.

Lovecraft's writing out of what Cardin calls *sehnsucht* (i.e., longing) leads the reader, first, to "the illusion of some strange suspension or violation of the galling limitations of time, space, and natural law which forever imprison us and frustrate our curiosity about the infinite cosmic spaces beyond the radius of our sight and analysis" (Cardin 120), which, second, leads to cosmic horror:

> Horror and the unknown or the strange are always closely connected, so that it is hard to create a convincing picture of shattered natural law or cosmic al-

---

8. Rick Elmore notes Ligotti's emphasis on pessimism as a "temperament" one is born into, an observation that fits with Ligotti's list. (Elmore, "Loving Rust's Pessimism.")

ienage or "outsideness" without laying stress on the emotion of fear. (Cardin 120, quoting Lovecraft *Miscellaneous Writings* 113)

The path between desire and horror is that of *sehnsucht* leading to an encounter with suspended or violated natural law, which then leads to cosmic horror.

Even though at one point he found himself feeling deep personal identification with Lovecraft, Ligotti understands his independence from Lovecraft. In an interview for *Eldritch Infernal,* Ligotti says:

> My aim is the opposite of Lovecraft's. He had an appreciation for natural scenery on earth and wanted to reach beyond the visible in the universe. I have no appreciation for natural scenery and want the objective universe to be a reflection of a character. (Satanis)

In some ways Ligotti is a natural bridge between Lovecraft and *True Detective*. In that series, the detectives, who come from similar cultures yet who possess radically different worldviews, represent these two poles. Rustin Cohle possesses a sensibility that would agree with having "an appreciation for natural scenery on earth" yet is someone who is philosophically opposed to simple, surface-level answers, while Martin Hart prefers the flat one-to-one correspondence between the objective and the subjective.

Ligotti's relationship with *True Detective* is a complex one, involving a deep relationship between the text and the television series and between Ligotti's words and Rustin Cohle's personal philosophy, all of which I address in chapter 3. As even the brief review above indicates, Lovecraft's genus-species relationship with Ligotti has been well documented by others, and Ligotti's importance to *True Detective* has been acknowledged by the series creator Nic Pizzolatto. Although for some pop culture commenters the series could not have existed without Ligotti, as I argue later in this study, without Lovecraft *True Detective* could not have existed in its current form, had it existed at all. Without Lovecraft's writing, Ligotti may have become a pessimist anyway, but can we know that? And could he have developed his own fiction and philosophy in the same way? The larger context of weird fiction would be radically different without Lovecraft as a writer and community member. Surely, at the very least, there would have been critical differences in that near-impossible timeline.

In light of what has been presented in this chapter so far, what new can be discovered about Ligotti's relationship with and connection to *True Detective*?

The basic elements have been established: pessimism as the foundation of Rust Cohle's philosophy, with Ligotti's take on pessimism as an accessible inroad to Rust's/Cohle's worldview. But as we have seen, both Ligotti's pessimism and Cohle's actions as motivated and shored up by pessimism are not as similar—and not as easy—as initially presented. Ligotti's pessimism runs into roadblocks, and Cohle's worldview has to shift as he finds that pessimism will obstruct his abilities as an investigator.

Cohle's full-throated embrace of pessimism in S1E1 is initially believable, even though it may not ring true with a given viewer's own worldview. As the Dora Lange investigation progresses and Cohle of necessity reveals more about his own past to Marty and, to a certain extent, to Hart's wife Maggie, pessimism becomes more contingent for Cohle. Even the brief, tenuous respite he feels after telling Marty and Maggie about his daughter's death and the loss of his marriage is enough to move Cohle into a different emotional/spiritual space, as Elmore observes ("Loving Rust's Pessimism" 112–13). From pessimism Cohle moves to fatalism, which gives Cohle "a negative but substantive meaning and purpose" ("Loving Rust's Pessimism" 113). This purpose enables Cohle to continue the investigation even after it was ostensibly solved and helps drive Cohle's to persuade Marty that, come what may, the two of them have to work together again if justice is to be served. Only once Cohle and Hart release their respective worldly concerns—Hart even gives his ex-wife a final goodbye before he and Cohle confront Errol Childress at the encampment—are they able to engage Childress without reserve. As the resident fatalist, Cohle's release involves his vowing never to look away again. Had Cohle clung to his pessimism, this vow and release may not have been possible.

As Ligotti insists in *Conspiracy,* some may find pessimism agreeable, but as a method for living even a simple life—not a life on the scale to which Cohle and Hart are forced to do—pessimism is a stop sign. Ligotti's brand of pessimism in *True Detective* fuels Cohle at the beginning, but it cannot carry Cohle through the end, and thus it blocks, obviates, deprives, degrades the possibility of justice. Pessimism makes a poor investigative tool, indeed.

Chapter 4: Signposts in H. P. Lovecraft toward *True Detective* and an Aesthetics of Investigation

"You think . . . you wonder, ever, if you're a bad man?"
"No, I don't wonder, Marty. The world needs bad men. We keep the other bad men from the door."
—*True Detective,* "The Locked Room," S1E3, 2014

Silent, her body kneeling beneath the wide arms of the ancient oak, her hands bound, her figure seemingly in prayer but praying to a pagan god who is pleased with the antlers resting on her still, dead scalp, the spiral drawn on her lower back drawing one of the detectives to examine her closely as he draws the scene in his notebook. This scene begins *True Detective,* which became famous for its use of the Book in season 1 (2014). To find our way through the woods of weird fiction and detective fiction so that we find the place in *True Detective* where Dora Lange's body waits kneeling under the tree, we will look at a brief review of the history of detective fiction, then look at two writers of tales of investigation—Edgar Allan Poe, who did it consciously, and Chambers, whose characters use investigative techniques in their pursuit of love and art. Both Poe and Chambers link to H. P. Lovecraft, whose narrators function frequently as investigators even when that is not their occupation.[1]

The investigator as a literary figure is a contentious one. Born out of traditions established by Edgar Allan Poe and Sir Arthur Conan Doyle, the investigator changed radically in twentieth-century detective fiction—moving from amateur to professional, investigator to criminal—and continues to change within the genre. As Christopher Pittard notes in his book *Purity and Contamina-*

---

1. This chapter was originally a paper presented at NecronomiCon Providence, August 2015.

tion in Late Victorian Detective Fiction, the investigator operates in the social margin because he has contact with criminals, with evil, and often with the very body of the victim (20). Similarly, Lovecraft's narrators move from center to margin and from social norms to cosmic horror. Lovecraft uses the same techniques as numerous detective fiction writers, a matter that I will address later. Without the investigator, without some figure fortified by curiosity and determination, much of Lovecraft's work would not have been possible.

Detective fiction's roots extend far back in literature, including such diverse narratives as the story of Bel and the Dragon in the biblical Book of Daniel (which is referenced by Reverend Joel Theriot in S1E3 of *True Detective,* "The Locked Room") and the story of Oedipus in *Oedipus Rex* (which is referenced in S2E1, "The Western Book of the Dead"). For example, in the story of Bel and the Dragon, Daniel reveals the methods of the false priests and, in so doing, reinforces the cultural position of those following western Christianity. Later, beloved detective Sherlock Holmes reinforces the norms and values of Victorian England in numerous stories. "The Man with the Twisted Lip" is a story about an ostensibly successful businessman, Neville St. Clair, who has in fact been earning a high income by posing as a beggar. Holmes agrees to keep St. Clair's secret so long as St. Clair discontinues his deceit. True to Victorian norms, the scandal is less that St. Clair has been deceiving his wife than that a beggar should earn a gentleman's income. Holmes's goal in his detective work is both to catch criminals and to shore up the values of the British Empire. He does not do it for fame or wealth, but for both the sake of the game and the good of British society. The function of detective fiction in culture has largely been to reinforce norms, a topic that I discuss in more detail in chapter 5.[2]

In the twentieth century, detective fiction changes in parallel with changes in philosophy and literature. Agatha Christie may have refined the parlor-game subgenre of detective fiction, but in *Curtain: Poirot's Last Case,* her final novel for

---

2. Gavin Callaghan notes in his discussion of Sherlock Holmes and Lovecraft, "It would indeed be ironic if it was *Holmes's own theory of human insignificance* that influenced Lovecraft in his decision to eschew not only realistic or compelling characters, but also the opportunity to create a heroic, recurring Holmes-like figure in his own tales. Holmes repeatedly berates Watson that he would rather solve his mysteries in anonymity. For him, the *work* is everything—*he* is nothing. Dr. Watson may have ignored Holmes's fictional advice, but *Lovecraft,* it appears, took it to heart" (Callaghan 201; emphasis in original).

Hercule Poirot, she makes him the murderer of a man who has committed no crimes himself. In the society-in-miniature of Christie's country-house mystery, the detective becomes the criminal, though in the service of society as a whole, a change that also appears in *True Detective*. In Christie's book, Poirot's victim Stephen Norton is a skilled manipulator of others, to the degree that persons kill or attempt to kill others after being in Norton's presence. Simply engaging in what seems nothing more than awkward yet casual conversation with Norton leads people to commit murder. Norton's powers of suggestion, masked by what seems to be his extreme social awkwardness, make him the perfect murderer by proxy.

Poirot recognizes Norton's technique, then sets up and executes the man's murder flawlessly. No one suspects Poirot. Four months after his own apparent heart attack and death, Poirot leaves a full, written confession as part of what is revealed to be his own suicide. Poirot kills Norton to protect society, then kills himself to right the wrong he committed. This action makes both Poirot and his victim societal scapegoats: as sacrifices, their deaths relieve the guilt of the society-in-miniature of the country-house genre. This idea of the necessity of sacrifice to relieve communal guilt is discussed at length by anthropologist René Girard and will be addressed later in this book.[3]

After World War II and the appearance of the hard-boiled detective, espionage fiction becomes its own genre within the context of the Cold War, deriving some techniques and dynamics from detective fiction while developing its own identity. An important parallel between espionage fiction and detective fiction is the triangular dynamic at its core, a powerhouse of tropes and ideas that drives other tropes and dynamics. The primary dynamic in espionage fiction is that of the lover, the beloved, and the interloper, which correspond to the handler, the spy, and the counterspy; in detective fiction, the triangular dynamic is that of the priest, the sacrifice, and the community, corresponding to the detective, the criminal, and society.[4]

Finally, by the end of the twentieth century, the recognition by writers of the limitations of human action and knowledge, which had been a part of more

---

3. Rene Girard's *Violence and the Sacred* is key to understanding the necessity of ritual violence in maintaining societal norms.

4. Girard devotes a fine degree of attention to his discussion of the dynamics of ritual sacrifice and societal absolution in *Violence and the Sacred*.

serious literary fiction, now begins appearing in detective fiction. The line between citizen and criminal becomes less sure. Following in Agatha Christie's footsteps, detectives become criminals themselves; clues become increasingly difficult to distinguish from their surroundings; and culprits' motives become clouded by the general murkiness of modernity. Today, detective fiction has expanded into new cultural contexts examining areas such as race, class, gender, postcolonialism, and other matters.

A look at the origins of modern detective fiction will be helpful for later discussion. Even though stories of investigation have appeared throughout Western literature, the genre officially begins with Edgar Allan Poe's short story "The Murders in the Rue Morgue" (1841). It is in his subsequent story "The Mystery of Marie Rogêt" (1842), however, where Poe outlines the process of creating a tale of ratiocination via footnotes and editorial comments. Poe's story's is a fictionalized version of an actual murder investigation, that of Mary Cecelia Rogers in New York. More importantly, it introduces the trope of the palimpsest into detective fiction, which will later become one of the central tropes of the genre. In this chapter I examine "The Mystery of Marie Rogêt" in the context of its place within early modern detective fiction and the tropes developed. In a later chapter I look at this story in the context of epistemological disorder.

The story opens with a quotation about suspension of disbelief that is similar to the manner in which some of Lovecraft's narrators will later begin their stories with a statement about believability. Gothic fiction and tropes are heavily influential, including Southern Gothic influences much as we see in *True Detective*,[5] and "The Mystery of Marie Rogêt" establishes some of the key tropes of detective fiction: clarity/obscurity, darkness/light, presence/absence, the discovery of the palimpsest of narratives, and the warring of narratives for dominance. Finally, though not thoroughly, Poe begins approaching an aesthetics of crime and investigation as he constructs the fictional narrative concerning Marie Rogêt that, as a palimpsest, overlays the actual narrative of Mary Rogers. The delicate sensibilities of detective C. Auguste Dupin and the aesthetics of the

---

5. For example, macabre events, criminal behavior, death, betrayal, and rural settings figure in both Gothic and Southern Gothic literature. A strong sense of place is present in both Southern Gothic and Southern literature in general, and Lovecraft presents an equally strong sense of place in his writings.

crime scene itself are key points in Dupin's discovery of the circumstances of Marie Rogêt's murder and the identity of the criminal.

The parallels between "The Mystery of Marie Rogêt" and Lovecraft's narratives in general are many. The mysteries are solved at a distance, using items such as newspaper accounts, diaries, cult-related texts, and other documents. This research is critical to the investigation. Both Poe's and Lovecraft's narrators perform a close analysis of all available evidence. In contrast with these narrators, the police in Poe and the scientific, medical, and legal communities in Lovecraft use poor thinking and judgment in their evaluation of the evidence. The narrator in "The Mystery of Marie Rogêt" is unnamed, and Lovecraft populates his stories with a number of nameless narrators. The stories move from a hidden narrative offered by an unreliable narrator to a revealed narrative that is adequately documented or otherwise proven. In "The Mystery of Marie Rogêt," when the narrator is called on by the public to reveal his findings, he chooses to do so; in Lovecraft, the narrators' motives vary, but often they decide on their own to come forth with their findings. Both authors provide as documentation items translated from other languages, even though in both authors' narratives the documentation is as fictional as the narratives they support, and certainly in Lovecraft's case the fictional documentation spurred other writers in his circle to use them creatively (Lauterbach 98). Finally, there is a struggle between narratives. In Poe, the struggle is between the accepted version, which has been published by newspaper reports and the police, and the narrator's version, which has been deduced by Dupin. In Lovecraft, the struggle between narratives is that of the narrator versus authorities and/or society, and aptly so: the core of detective fiction is the struggle between fictions, the layered narratives of the innocent and the guilty, the criminal and the detective, the community and the perpetrator.

Later detectives will sort through evidence as though solving a logic problem on a grid, but for Poe, Dupin uses exegesis to discover the truth about the murder. The key difference between the world in which Dupin functions and the worlds of Lovecraft and the *True Detective* investigators is that Dupin's world is a knowable one with no sense of cosmic horror. Dupin's solving of the murder of Marie Rogêt returns the community to a sense of safety and familiarity and normalizes the community ethos. Lovecraft's narrators, as well as Cohle and Hart in *True Detective,* can do neither.

An example of how the safe and familiar are permanently violated post-Poe is in Lovecraft's "The Call of Cthulhu" (1926). The plot elements of "The Call of Cthulhu" are similar to those of standard detective fiction. The death of a relative brings the narrator into the story. As executor of the estate, the narrator examines the deceased's possessions, finds some oddities, and investigates. The investigation leads to more questions, then initial answers are gathered, and the narrator's review of the assembled evidence provides fuller explanations. What makes the difference is Lovecraft's use of cosmicism and cosmic horror.

Just as a detective pieces together clues and constructs a narrative, the narrator of "The Call of Cthulhu," Francis Wayland Thurston, pieces together clues and constructs a glimpse of the cult of worshippers surrounding the figure of Cthulhu. By his own account, Thurston first glimpses the truth about the cult and its leader when he "fleshed out from an accidental piecing together of separated things—in this case an old newspaper item and the notes of a dead professor" (*CF* 2.22). This collation of a variety of sources, including among other items dream journals, a dead sailor's monograph, interviews with a police detective from New Orleans, and a mysterious stone statuette, leads to Thurston's understanding not only of the existence of Cthulhu and his cult, but also of Thurston's own approaching demise at the hands of a cult member.

The final mystery in the story is Thurston's imminent death. Thurston knows his death at the hands of the Cthulhu cult is assured, given the suspicious deaths of the others investigating the cult. Lovecraft uses the many threads of the story to construct a palimpsest of narratives: the arrival of Cthulhu and others on our planet is overlaid by Cthulhu's entombment; the subsequent development of the cult through dream messages from Cthulhu as he sleeps; and the passing down of the cult through generations which as a layer is overlaid by the murders in the Louisiana swamps; the sudden re-emergence of dreams and other phenomena in sensitives such as the artist Henry Anthony Wilcox, who creates a bas-relief sculpture of Cthulhu that was inspired by a dream; and the investigation by Inspector Legrasse and Thurston are both overlaid by Thurston's ultimate collection of the evidence and his apprehension of cosmic horror as he understands the full story.

"The Dunwich Horror" (1928) is another Lovecraft story with a central figure investigating strange events. We read of external documentation of the

Whateley residence and its associated peculiarities, this time from three sources: government officers, government medical experts, and newspaper reporters. Next, Dr. Henry Armitage launches his investigation after Wilbur Whateley arouses his suspicions. Armitage collects all the available data about Wilbur and the goings-on in Dunwich, then talks with Dr. Houghton of Aylesbury about Old Whateley's death. Armitage next visits Dunwich to see for himself the remaining evidence. After his return to Miskatonic, Armitage reads the passages in the *Necronomicon* that were of interest to Wilbur. Armitage then speaks with students of the occult in Boston and elsewhere. Finally, Armitage collates the available information and begins to understand the cosmic horror that has come to Dunwich. Once Armitage decides to act, he enlists the aid of Professor Warren Rice and Dr. Francis Morgan. Together, they confront the cosmic horror of the Whateley family and, after repelling it, partially restore the social norms of the tiny community. In addition to using many of the tropes and dynamics of detective fiction, Lovecraft uses cosmic horror to upend the seemingly normal narrative of detection and investigation.

Through the use of these tropes, dynamics, and other devices, detective fiction is rich in its development as a genre as it parallels developments in twentieth-century Western thought. James Arthur Anderson's book *Out of the Shadows* serves as an easy introduction to structuralist analysis of Lovecraft's works. For our purposes, Anderson's elucidation of binary relationships—one of the key methodologies of structuralism—helps us start examining tropes in detective fiction.[6] Rather than taking a deep dive into structuralism, I will offer a single, signal quote from Anderson that may help illuminate later discussions:

> [P]oststructuralist theory realizes that attempting to substitute the word for the actual object creates "slippage," which leads to a deconstructing of the text . . . Horror and weird fiction, of course, rely upon this slippage as part of their premise. (82–83)

---

6. Revelation/concealment is arguably the dominant dynamic in detective fiction. Just as the detective struggles to reveal what the perpetrator or criminal wants to conceal, the author navigates between revealing enough for the sake of fair play—a critical point among devotees of detective fiction—and keeping details concealed so that the final revelation is still a surprise for the reader. From revelation and concealment come many of the other paired tropes, especially those related to vision.

This kind of slippage is incredibly important for detective fiction as well. Without it, the lacunae between the author and the reader would not exist. Detective fiction authors use this slippage to deceive the reader—and note that it is a reader *who wishes to be deceived temporarily*—to create false trails, red herrings, and dead ends. The re-establishment of the text and correction of the slippage is the basis of detective fiction; it is the solving of the crime and the revelation of the criminal and his plot. Similarly, though horror and weird fiction may not always have a tidy resolution (and today's detective fiction does not necessarily, either), the quest itself through the weird is arguably still as important.

In addition to the tropes established by Poe in "The Mystery of Marie Rogêt" outlined above, another is that of the mask. Masking/unmasking is key to Chambers's stories in the Book. Characters struggle with the social masks they are required to wear in light of the desires they feel for love, sex, and freedom. Within this context, the Play references masking and unmasking in the chapter "The Mask," which draws on "Cassilda's Song," the opening lines of Chambers's book and purportedly a quotation from the Play:

> CAMILLA: You, sir, should unmask.
> STRANGER: Indeed?
> CASSILDA: Indeed, it's time. We all have laid aside disguise but you.
> STRANGER: I wear no mask.
> CAMILLA: (Terrified, aside to Cassilda.) No mask? No mask! (Chambers, *Yellow Sign* 33)

Once the characters in the Book read the text-within-the-text, they are socially unmasked, less able to fit within society's constraints. Other characters in the Book, such as those in the vignettes in the chapter "The Prophets' Paradise," struggle with the way our masks obstruct us in our search to understand love, death, and beauty. For Chambers's characters throughout the Book, love and art are interchangeable, and it is the heightened sensibilities of the artist that make fuller access to love possible and help them in their investigative pursuits. At the same time, each chapter of Chambers's book is about loss in some way, and thus absence. These are all key elements of the detective's makeup in detective fiction.

Aesthetic sensibilities derived from artistic training form the basis of the characters' successes as quasi-investigators. Chambers's central characters—

largely painters, but sometimes those involved in other arts, such as sculpture and theatre—have aesthetic sensibilities available only to those with training in the arts. Most of the chapters of the Book involve an encounter with beauty, such as the Sylvia in "The Street of the First Shell" or Trent's encounter with war in the same story, or the Sylvia of "The Street of the Four Winds," who is only a memory to the narrator Severn. It is through beauty that the narrators discover love. Their sense of aesthetics leads them to investigate moments of intensified beauty. Chambers's narrators would seem to be highly conventional figures, then, but for the presence of the Play: it destroys lives, upends cultures, and provokes the power of the authorities. The curiosity and determination possessed by Chambers's narrators both moves them toward love and, in some instances, toward madness and death when that same curiosity and determination, along with the power of the very text of the play, lures them into the realm of the Yellow King. It is these heightened artistic sensibilities that figure so strongly for both Lovecraft's narrators and the figure of Rustin Cohle in *True Detective*.

Lovecraft's narrators, who are from a relatively narrow set of occupations (when specified at all), possess the curiosity, courage, and determination that are key to development of artistic sensibilities. In *At the Mountains of Madness* (1931), the narrator Dyer traces the history of the Great Old Ones through bas-reliefs and begins to understand the scope and development of the Old Ones' civilization, as well as the kind of formidable opponents they represent. Dyer's grasp of the meaning of the bas reliefs is central to the revelations to come; his determination to survive and warn others drives his retelling of the Antarctic expedition once he returns home.

Similarly, the narrator in "The Music of Erich Zann" (1921) is not a musician himself but is instead someone who has an educated appreciation for it. It is this appreciation that leads him to the door of the viol player Zann and to the mind-rending discoveries therein. Zann's apartment window does not display a cityscape, as it properly should; instead, it reveals an opening into space, possibly into a different dimension. For Lovecraft, unlike Chambers, aesthetic sensibilities can lead beyond mere encounters with beauty to encounters with cosmic horror. But for the narrator's sensitivity to the beauty of Zann's viol playing, Zann might have survived the end of the narrator's story, and the narrator might have remained innocent, though less well-informed. Instead, the encounter between Zann and the narrator leads to death (*CF* 2.280–90). Other of Lovecraft's narrators, such as Thurber in "Pickman's Model" (1926; *CF* 2.56–72) follow similar aesthetic instincts. Had Thurber not possessed those instincts, he wouldn't have seen Pickman's paintings and learned the truth about both Pickman and his model. Thurber himself notes that "only the real artist knows the actual anatomy of the terrible or the physiology of fear" (*CF* 2.57), thus affirming the link between aesthetics and encounters with the extramundane.

The aesthetic is the core for Poe, Chambers, and Lovecraft. In Poe, we have such a figure in Dupin, who is an aesthete even among Parisian aesthetes, given the lineage of the aesthete in the Decadent movement.[7] In Chambers, we have artists who follow leads, track down people, and discover the truth behind numerous sets of mysterious circumstances, sometimes going mad in the process. In Lovecraft, we have a wide variety of narrators who end up investigating circumstances and events of all kinds.

The investigator must understand his investigation as an epistemology—as an examination of how what is known has come to be known—so that he understands both where the boundaries have been laid by others and the limits of his own perceptions and experiences. Thus, part of the work of the investigator involves an epistemology of investigation. It is not enough for an investigator simply to claim to know something; to know how he knows it is as important as knowing why he needs to know it. Richard Foley, in his article "An Epistemology That Matters," notes, "The two most fundamental questions for an epistemology are, what is involved in having good reasons to believe a claim, and what is involved in meeting the higher standard of knowledge that a claim is true?" (1). In a police procedural such as *True Detective*, epistemology and teleology cannot be separated. That is to say, how the detectives know something—how they claim that something is known and significant—cannot be separated from their purpose in knowing it. The teleological ends of goodness, betterness, and value—elements that affirm that something is worth knowing—cannot be separated from the deontological ends of rightness, obligation, and duty. The ends of investigation cannot be separated from the duty of the investigator. Thus, investigation is innately both epistemological and teleologi-

---

7. The Decadent movement is fascinating and, alas, too much of a diversion to examine in depth in this study.

cal: it is the duty of the investigator to find out what is worth knowing and follow it to its ends.

The context for discussion of the epistemology of investigation is usually within the realm of criminal law and legal theory. However, its core questions are appropriately discussed here. The epistemology of investigation has as its basic question,

> Does the criminal investigation rise to the level of scientific investigation? That is, is it a truth-finding pursuit—if not, it is little better than a witch hunt—and is it normative, i.e., can narrative values be attached to behaviour and attribute responsibility to the persons involved in the behaviour under investigation? (Zeegers)

If the above questions can be answered with a "yes," then there is a basis for the epistemology of an investigation. This is why the detective as a literary figure and the detectives in *True Detective* all wrestle with moral issues as well as criminal ones: normative values are often, though not always, the same as moral ones, and moral issues become communal and societal issues.

How, then, does the investigator approach this necessity for an epistemology? Through the aesthetics of crime, investigation, and redemption as they are functions of narrative and normative systems. In other words, the ways that the community is redeemed through the investigation of crime and the punishment of criminals is what helps fashion the aesthetics of the investigation. This aesthetic points to the epistemology used as part of the investigation. Perhaps the most notable investigator possessing a fine aesthetic is Sherlock Holmes, with his appreciation of music and his aptitude for disguise, and certainly his extreme intellectuality in his approach to crime solving. Another one would be Dupin, Poe's detective, who combines ratiocination with his own creative imagination. Both of these detectives use their aesthetic sensibilities in their crime solving: aesthetics becomes a tool through which the detective perceives what others are missing and by which he gains understanding of the criminal and his motivation.

These things, then, require development at this point: the aesthetics of crime, the aesthetics of investigation, and the aesthetics of redemption. Discussions of the aesthetics of criminality go back as far as Jack the Ripper. Simon Joyce in his essay "Sexual Politics and the Aesthetics of Crime" notes that readers during the late nineteenth century had available to them both works of popular fiction, such as Sir Arthur Conan Doyle's detective tales, and newspaper stories of Jack the Ripper, the exploits of whom became increasingly compared to Robert Louis Stevenson's novella *The Strange Case of Dr. Jekyll and Mr. Hyde* (502), as well as to familiar villains found in both legends and Gothic fiction. These events and fictions became part of the public imagination, leading to a strong narrative understanding of crime. Here, a criminal's activity forms a narrative, and his skill as a criminal becomes a set of aesthetic criteria, with more skilled criminals having a better reputation among the public and, perhaps, the authorities. One can imagine police and detectives with a grudging acceptance of, if not admiration for, a highly professional thief. The aesthetic of redemption for the criminal who is still on the loose is the aggregation of successful criminal acts, possibly to include trophies from victims, items that would then remind the criminal of his freedom from societal norms.

The aesthetics of investigation follows that of police procedure, where the normative function of the legal system creates a structure by which evidence can be evaluated and criminals can be charged with crimes. The narrative of a given crime becomes the background of the narrative of police activity. The aesthetics of investigation involves thorough collection of evidence, analysis of its significance, and reconstruction of the crime narrative. The investigator's special skills in perception form the basis of the investigative aesthetic. A highly developed investigative aesthetic would be indicated by a detective's knowledge of details and fine understanding of the criminal mind.

The aesthetics of redemption involves the story of the redeemed criminal, that is, how the criminal was at one time, what happened to change him, and how he is different now. These aesthetics also involve the investigator and the community. The criminal's personal narrative forms the basis of his story of redemption, and the quality, nuance, and authenticity of his narrative inform the aesthetic judgment of it. The investigators redeem the community in the biblical sense of the redemption of the people: the investigators catch the criminal to buy the freedom of the community. The freedom of the community depends on the simultaneous existence and imprisonment of the criminal. If the criminal has not been captured, the community cannot be redeemed, because the criminal within its ranks actions as a contaminant.

All these matters, from the tropes established by Poe to the aesthetics of the investigator, are important components of the world of Rustin Cohle and

Martin Hart in *True Detective*. Cohle and Hart are different in almost every way, especially in terms of their differing aesthetics. Hart's personal aesthetic operates out of a similar sense of loss and absence to that of the conventional detective, especially the hard-boiled detective. Hart has all the external evidence of a successful life: a beautiful wife, two daughters, a home, a good job as police investigator, and the usual testosterone-laced relationships with his fellow officers. But Hart is a womanizer who seeks to fill his growing feelings of emptiness with sexual relationships. Unable to resist advances from women, his adulterous liaisons do not offer him a way out of his core isolation.

When his life falls apart after his mistress tells his wife of their affair, Hart retreats even deeper into the conventional world by dropping his sexual liaisons and finding religion. Ultimately, his efforts fail because he does not understand himself or his core aesthetic of deceit and entitlement—even at the end, in S1E8, when his now ex-wife and daughters visit him in the hospital after the death of Errol Childress, Hart lies to them again, telling them that everything will be all right. Despite his reassurances, he knows that he and Cohle cannot stop the cult of the King in Yellow because its political and social connections run too deep in southern Louisiana. Hart's aesthetic remains one of deceit and corruption masked by assurances of conventionality.

Despite the emotional inadequacies of his life, Hart is supremely comfortable with keeping up the façade of family man and social conformist. Even his infidelity is simply another conventional item, merely kept secret; his public and his secret life mesh thoroughly with his social and cultural milieu. The hollow moral didacticism he offers his children is a poor attempt to guide his daughters on a path he cannot follow himself. Hart's lives—both of them—are empty, hollow, conformist, and conventional.

Interestingly, Hart uses this conventionality—his "regular guy" persona—to throw the police department's internal affairs investigators, Gilbaugh and Papania, off his track. In "The Secret Fate of All Life," he tells the two men, "I tell it the same way that I told the shooting board and every cop bar between Houston and Biloxi. And you know why the story is always the same seventeen years gone? Because it only went down the one way" (S1E5). Hart knows that the investigators will probably find his version reliable because it agrees with the findings of the shooting board, a higher authority than Hart alone.

During this sequence, the creators of *True Detective* employ the technique of the palimpsest—overwriting, as it were, the original sequences of the shooting at the LeDoux encampment with the sequences of the narrative that Hart and Cohle gave to the shooting board—to misdirect Gilbaugh and Papania in their investigation of Cohle. The palimpsest is portrayed visually through sequences of Cohle and Hart at the LeDoux encampment shootout—which shows the audience what "really happened"—that are intercut with their calm, reasoned testimony before the shooting board, which presents a very different version of events at the encampment.

The bridge between Hart and Cohle is, ironically, the Play. As Lovecraft warns us in "The Call of Cthulhu," "The most merciful thing in the world, I think, is the inability of the human mind to correlate all its contents" (*CF* 2.21). This is what the Play does in Chambers's work. It is also what the idea of the Yellow King ultimately does in *True Detective*: it forces Cohle and Hart to correlate the evidence and discover horrible things. The Yellow King is never revealed in *True Detective*, yet his power drives Errol Childress and other members of the cult to torture and murder, just as he drives Cohle to continue investigating. In fact, it is the very name "The Yellow King," used by Guy Leonard Francis during his own interrogation in S1E5, "The Secret Fate of All Life," that brings Cohle back into the investigation. The Yellow King wrecks Cohle's life by driving his obsession; at the same time the Yellow King wrecks Hart's life by bringing him local fame that ultimately wrecks his family, largely by making Hart unwilling to resist women.

In contrast with Hart, and to use a section of Lovecraft's essay "Supernatural Horror in Literature" (1925–27) as a palimpsest for a reading of Cohle's character (*CE* 2.100–101), Cohle's impartiality is what makes him a great investigator and interrogator, yet it is also what keeps him from being intimate with others. He is the vivid and detached chronicler of crimes and crime scenes. He is neither teacher nor sympathizer (although he convinces the suspects he interrogates that he is sympathetic), and the only opinions he vends are his own—and only when asked. Cohle sees life and thought as rightful considerations during any given investigation. His work requires that he interpret powerful feelings and happenings that attend crimes, that he see the decay, terror, adversity, and indifference of victims and criminals, that he disregard the taste and traditional outward sentiments of humanity, and that he sacrifice his own health, sanity, and normal expansive welfare for the sake of the community.

As Fritz Leiber famously said of Lovecraft, Cohle is a Copernicus in *True Detective*. Leiber says that Lovecraft "shifted the focus of supernatural dread from man and his little world and his gods, to the stars and the black and unplumbed gulfs of intergalactic space. To do this effectively, he created a new kind of horror story and new methods for telling it" (50). Cohle does this in *True Detective* with the social and cultural iconography of southern Louisiana. He re-centers the dialogue so that Marty Hart and others are forced to look at the world from a position different from their native understanding. This ability to resituate the narrative is also why those around him are resistant to his ideas: through his intellectual and philosophical prowess, Cohle invokes similar "black and unplumbed gulfs."

Given that human significance is so limited, one would wonder why Cohle stays with the murder cases. One reason would be because of their weird tale elements, specifically the philosophy and aesthetic of the events. The cult of the Yellow King has adopted a set of beliefs that removes it from conventional thinking and action, that is, it has created for itself the environment of the weird tale, with Chambers's book providing the folkloric spine. Cohle comes to recognize this in his own terms first as a police investigator, then as a private citizen. In a scene in "The Locked Room," Cohle tells the detectives,

> This [patting folder with photo of latest victim]. This is what I'm talking about. This is what I mean when I'm talking about time and death and futility. That there are broader ideas at work, mainly what is owed between us as a society for our mutual illusions. (S1E3)

Just as with Danforth in *At the Mountains of Madness,* Cohle possesses the vulnerabilities associated with the artistic temperament: heightened awareness, a gift for connecting things that are not obvious, and an awareness of the aesthetics of a given situation that might be related to the aesthetics of another, that is, a trans-aesthetic sensitivity.

Cohle's aesthetic is that of an artist who seeks to understand and see before he begins to work and whose ultimate act of seeing is to capture a perpetrator and gain his confession. As an example, in S1E1, "The Long Bright Dark," Cohle brings a ledger to the scene where the body of Dora Lange was left to be discovered—Cohle's nickname from another police force, as it turns out, is "Tax Man"—and in it Cohle documents evidence, findings, leads, and numerous other items related to the investigation, including drawings of the murder victim Dora Lange and the devil nets surrounding her body. For now, the investigation seems to remain within normal limits, despite the odd elements around Lange's body. Things change the more the detectives learn, however, and soon, exposure to these new ideas leads to their mental disarray, just as in *At the Mountains of Madness* (1931) the oppressive polar solitude, paired with sights inducing cosmic horror, leads to the mental disarray of Dyer and ultimately to the insanity of Danforth. What keeps Cohle and Hart (and Dyer/Danforth) on the level is a mutual agreement about there being a plausible explanation involving human agency.

Later, in the episode "After You've Gone" (S1E7), Hart joins Cohle in Cohle's storage unit, which he has turned into an artist's studio of sorts, filled with drawings, maps, documents, and all the evidence that Cohle could assemble as a civilian, arranged as a collage on the surfaces of the storage unit. As Anderson notes in *Out of the Shadows*, "In a strange sort of textual code of its own, the horror story becomes a metaphor for the quest for knowledge—even though we know it may not be pleasant, so does it attract and seduce in its own perverse way" (87). Similarly, Cohle's storage-unit-as-atelier helps him to begin correlating what he knows about the cult, the murders, and the victims.

As an investigator, Cohle sorts his personal beliefs by removing the human and focusing on the realm of ideas. Human insignificance in the cosmos is the basis of his philosophical beliefs, which in turn forms the basis of his aesthetic as an investigator.[8] Cohle tells Gilbaugh and Papania in S1E3, "The Locked Room,"

> I've seen the finale of thousands of lives. Each one is so sure of their realness. That their sensory experience constituted a unique individual with purpose, meaning. So certain that they were more than a biological puppet. The truth wills out, and everybody sees that once the strings are cut off, all fall down.

As S. T. Joshi notes in "Lovecraft Criticism: A Study," "This reflexion of man's ludicrously minute position in the cosmos is perpetually conveyed in [Lovecraft's] fiction, and may perhaps be Lovecraft's major contribution to lit-

---

8. Thomas Ligotti's *The Conspiracy against the Human Race*, while not appropriate for this discussion of detective fiction, is illuminating with regard to Rustin Cohle's personal philosophy and is discussed in chapter 3.

erature" (20–21). The grasp of the utter meaninglessness of human agency in both Lovecraft and *True Detective* is part of the keystone that makes Lovecraft the critical part in the path from Chambers to *True Detective*. In *True Detective*, normal, garden-variety people have no way of withstanding the actions of those in positions of power. The cult members are so highly placed in local society that they enjoy perpetual protection.[9] Despite this powerlessness, Cohle affirms the power of right action at the end of S1E8, "Form and Void," when he announces to Hart that he believes the light of the stars is winning the battle against the darkness of space.

Yet one question remains: can we say that there really is such a thing as a true detective? There is substantial doubt, especially in light of the development of detective fiction since the middle of the twentieth century. Hart and Cohle are both Janus figures. Hart is duplicitous yet seen as trustworthy; Cohle has integrity and is brutally honest, but none of his fellow officers trust or even like him. Hart's strengths are in police procedure work; he is rough, unrefined, and knows how to work a suspect over. He has tremendous skill in ferreting out leads and details. Still, Hart is too much of a conformist to fit into the worlds that Cohle inhabits.

By the end of season 1, Hart is a private investigator, a gumshoe detective, estranged from his family and on tenuous terms with his former colleagues on the police force. Cohle, on the other hand, resembles a gumshoe detective in some ways, but he does not embrace the role. He is rejected, dismissed, an outsider to both his fellow police officers and the civilians who know him. He is brilliant and has no problem demonstrating that to his fellow officers, which they resent. He is more experienced in detective and undercover work than they are, and he also "knows some moves," as Hart puts it (S1E3, "The Locked Room"). He is an interrogator supreme, the best "box man" in the state (S1E5, "The Secret Fate of All Life"). In contrast with Hart, Cohle doesn't fit in among other cops and only just fits in as a police investigator. His natural milieu is the nighttime, that of the noir detective, as demonstrated by his easy burglary of Reverend Tuttle's home (S1E7, "After You've Gone"). To paraphrase from Dirk Mosig's article "H. P. Lovecraft: Myth-Maker," *True Detective* does similar

---

9. The same sense of the powerlessness of normal people, those who are not wealthy and well-connected, is a driving force behind season 2 of *True Detective* and, to a certain extent, to season 3.

things with human relationships and society that Lovecraft does with cosmic horror (111). The world of *True Detective* is mechanistic and materialistic. It illustrates realms within normal life that exist in front of everyone yet are nevertheless unseen. We normal, everyday people are in a laughable position in both the cosmos and in our own neighborhoods; we are powerless to affect the circumstances in which we find ourselves.

So who is the true detective? Is it possible for there to be such a person anymore, given the many changes in culture, police procedure, philosophy, and the legal system that have taken place since the first of Poe's stories was published? Perhaps the answer is in the section of dialogue between Hart and Cohle from "The Locked Room" (S1E3), quoted at the beginning of this chapter:

"You think . . . you wonder, ever, if you're a bad man?"

"No, I don't wonder, Marty. The world needs bad men. We keep the other bad men from the door."

Chapter 5: H. P. Lovecraft and the Dynamics of Detective Fiction

> Assuming I was sane and awake, my experience on that night was such as has befallen no man before. Mercifully there is no proof, for in my fright I lost the awesome object which would—if real and brought out of that noxious abyss—have formed irrefutable evidence.
> —Nathaniel Wingate Peaslee in "The Shadow out of Time"

As a man struggling to discover the truth about his past, Nathaniel Wingate Peaslee in "The Shadow out of Time" (1934–35) becomes a detective on his own trail. His slowly returning memories, which he relives during his exploration of the city of the Great Race of Yith beneath the Australian desert, bolster the evidence he has collected from his readings on amnesiac episodes. That investigation of the underground city leads him to a library shelf containing conclusive, damning evidence: his own handwriting on the pages of an impossibly old book. Intending to take the book to his son at their above-ground camp, Peaslee is discovered and pursued by the creatures the Yithians most feared. During his escape, Peaslee loses the only evidence proving that his mental journeys with the Yithians took place, yet he is simultaneously relieved by the loss. In the quotation introducing this chapter, we see key elements of detective fiction—investigation, collection of evidence, and explanation of events—turned by Lovecraft to his own purposes.[1]

Scholars frequently treat Lovecraft's narrators as a doorway to the study of cosmic horror, which is entirely reasonable. However, they less frequently study narrators as investigators, and the critical literature does not offer extensive analysis of Lovecraft's use of detective fiction tropes and conventions. This gap in knowledge prevents us from understanding the energy these elements bring to

---

1. This chapter was originally presented at NecronomiCon Providence, August 2017.

Lovecraft's fiction. Rather than simply patterning his stories after those of detective fiction writers, Lovecraft's use of the genre's tropes energizes his stories and helps amplify the form and structure of his brand of weird fiction. Rather than merely being influenced by this or that author, Lovecraft's use of detective fiction tropes and dynamics suggests a more adaptive approach by him. This chapter looks at how those tropes and dynamics work in Lovecraft's weird fiction.

As previously noted, detective fiction's roots include such diverse narratives as the story of Bel and the Dragon in the biblical Book of Daniel (Daniel 14:1–22) and the story of Oedipus in *Oedipus the King*. The function of detection in culture has largely been to reinforce social norms and affirm social conventions, whether the inciting incident is a mystery or a crime.[2] Between the biblical and Greek examples above and the better-known works of late Victorian and early twentieth-century detective fiction lie works by authors such as Wilkie Collins, whose novel *The Moonstone* (1868) is widely cited as the first English detective novel. Its roots in Gothic horror make *The Moonstone* a significant influence on numerous writers, and its plot involving a mystery, rather than a crime, is highly influential.[3]

Lovecraft would have been well aware of these late Victorian writers who produced detective fiction; Sir Arthur Conan Doyle published most of his Sherlock Holmes stories during his lifetime.[4] Lovecraft discusses some works by Algernon Blackwood and William Hope Hodgson and mentions J. Sheridan Le Fanu in passing in his essay "Supernatural Horror in Literature," evaluating in a

---

2. Authors and critics of detective fiction debate the use of the terms "mystery" versus "crime" in the genre and whether detective fiction properly fits one of the two. Larry Landrum and Christopher Pittard, both discussed later, address this from different points of view.
3. Larry Landrum and Dorothy Sayers, the latter a popular and highly respected writer of detective fiction herself, are just two among many who cite the importance of Collins's novel within the genre. *The Moonstone* is a common jumping-off point for a discussion of the history of detective fiction; given the length and depth of the genre, an extensive history of it would take more space than this work allows.
4. *A Study in Scarlet*, the first Sherlock Holmes novel, was published in 1887, only 3 years before Lovecraft was born, and the second novel, *The Sign of Four*, was published February 1890, 6 months before Lovecraft's birth. The first Holmes short story, "A Scandal in Bohemia," was published 25 June 1891 in the July issue of *The Strand* magazine. Doyle's final Holmes story was published in 1927, when Lovecraft was 37 years old.

general way the effectiveness of detective fiction elements.[5] Although occasional works before Poe's time have some, but not all, of the elements of detective fiction, Poe is the writer who brings the elements together.

The ground laid by these early authors and others made possible the works of Sir Arthur Conan Doyle (1859–1930), whose novel *A Study in Scarlet* (1887) introduced the world to Sherlock Holmes. Concealment of untidy truths is a key element of preserving social mores and class constraints, and in Lovecraft it becomes an important prop to the existing social, scientific, governmental, and cultural orders.[6]

Another important influence on nineteenth-century detectives is the relationship of Gothic horror to race. As Keen notes, the Gothic has its roots in racial insecurity:

> [C]ritics, particularly those focusing on the later nineteenth-century gothic revival, see in it a convenient imaginative space in which to work out guilt about mistreating other races and appropriating their lands (while allowing the continuance of the profitable British adventure) . . . In accordance with the Manichaean logic now strongly associated with Orientalism as described by Edward Said, an English self-understanding arises out of the characterization of exotic difference and depravity. (71)

---

5. A fuller discussion of "Supernatural Horror" can be found later in this work.
6. The revelation of what was concealed is part of the thrill of the genre, with its origins in Gothic fiction. As Suzanne Keen notes in her study *Romances of the Archive in Contemporary British Fiction,* "The intense feeling with which characters respond to revelations about the past carries over from eighteenth- and nineteenth-century gothic and sensation fiction into contemporary mystery thrillers and the Lovecraftian sub-genre called gothic horror . . . secrets of hidden messages in boxes, chests, and cabinets (or other pieces of furniture with concealed compartments) . . . [and finding them] may endanger the life or sanity of the quester. The unspeakable contents or occult power of the letters, diaries, scraps, recipes, maps, or suggestive lists contained in gothic hiding-places unleash hazardous knowledge about the past that is often better off contained, sealed, buried, or cast in a crevasse" (70–71). For Lovecraft's purposes, the location of the hidden secrets is less significant—sometimes only slightly so—than the contents themselves. The thrill of the discovery is primary; location is secondary to message. The revelation of the contents does indeed endanger life and sanity in Lovecraft; the contents unleash hazardous knowledge as in Gothic fiction, but of the present and the future as well as of the past. Human history as a construct is shaken by the discoveries Lovecraft's narrators make.

English identity, and by extension the identity of white European writers, was in some ways defined by the other. Extending this to Lovecraft, the self-as-narrator sometimes worries about losing his humanity in the face, however obliquely presented, of the encountered horror. For example, in "The Horror at Red Hook," the detective Malone rejects the minorities he sees in the Red Hook neighborhood as he investigates the cult. Malone's struggle is not only with the cultists and their leaders; his own race-based distaste for the cult's practitioners, who are largely if not entirely minorities, is a significant part of the narrative.[7]

By the twentieth century, detective fiction changes again, this time in parallel with changes in philosophy and literature.[8] Agatha Christie may have refined the parlor-game subgenre of detective fiction during the Golden Age, but in *Curtain: Poirot's Last Case,* her final novel for Hercule Poirot, she makes him both savior and defiler. As Christopher Pittard notes in his book *Purity and Contamination in Late Detective Fiction,*

> [T]he fictional detective . . . became an outcast, a link between crime and society who, by the nature of his task, had to work alone in order to protect his community from the taint of criminality. With the arrival of the detective, society was able to separate itself from the taint of criminality, but as a result the detective himself would be condemned to a life of crime. (146)

Even though investigators may be outliers—some through societal distrust, others self-imposed—many detectives do not work alone. The detective's sidekick, a figure such as Arthur Hastings for Poirot and John Watson for Holmes, functions as both an audience foil and a normative voice. In contrast to their sidekicks, detectives such as Poirot and Holmes are both within and without society, liminal figures traversing the border between law and crime, a

---

7. Numerous authors address issues of race and ethnicity in Lovecraft's works. This subject, like that of occult detectives, has become its own industry and cannot be adequately covered in this article.

8. Within Lovecraftiana, new developments expand on these changes. Occult detectives, like those in J. Sheridan Le Fanu and others, have experienced a revival and are now a minor industry within Lovecraft studies. The number of books, stories, graphic novels, and the like that have occult detective protagonists has exploded during the past few years. A full discussion of them is a study in itself and is beyond the scope of this work; however, Darrell Schweitzer notes that Lovecraft specifically has no ongoing main characters and thus no occult detectives (24).

border repeatedly negotiated by those sidekicks (Pittard 20).[9]

These elements of influence are important to keep in mind when looking at Lovecraft and detective fiction. To arrive at Lovecraft's use of the genre's conventions, however, we will need to return to Edgar Allan Poe. Not only is Poe a writer whom Lovecraft admired since boyhood, he is also widely credited with the creation of the modern short story, as well as the creation of the first detective fiction short story, "The Murders in the Rue Morgue."[10] Although most critics examine "Rue Morgue" in detail, for purposes of this analysis, the story "The Mystery of Marie Rogêt" is better suited.[11]

Poe's significance in Lovecraft's development cannot be overemphasized. Lovecraft sets aside Poe's tales of ratiocination in his essay "Supernatural Horror in Literature" (*CE* 2.102) before laying out Poe's influence on his own sense of weird fiction. The critical new element Poe offered, according to Lovecraft, is the use of psychological elements rather than moral ones as the core of the examination of the human psyche (*CE* 2.101). Poe reoriented horror away from moral obligations to the reader and toward a psychological realism rarely employed as a primary method by earlier writers of horror and Gothic fiction. After analyzing some of Poe's works, Lovecraft concludes that "Poe's weird tales are *alive* in a manner that few others can ever hope to be" (*CE* 2.103; emphasis in original).

---

9. This is especially true of the hard-boiled detective, a literary product very much of the 20th century, but the shifting status of the detective long precedes it. Police forces were first established in the 19th century, and public objections to them were common, especially in England. As Pittard notes, "Before the founding of the Metropolitan Police in 1829 and the detective department in 1842, detection was seen doubly as both the intrusive power of the state and as foreign, un-English espionage . . . The detective, on the margins of respectable society, was a liminal figure . . . 'To have been at the margins is to have been in contact with danger, to have been at a source of power.' If detectives cleansed social dirt, then some of that mess moved onto them" (20). In terms of "mess," Lovecraft's investigators, if they are exceedingly lucky, escape encounters with only the memory of cosmic horror and slip back into quiet lives, even though some, such as Francis Wayland Thurston in "The Call of Cthulhu," know that an unpleasant end awaits them. What matters to these investigators is that the truth has been revealed, even if only once, and even if it is buried again to protect society.

10. Three of his tales of ratiocination were published during a four-year period. The first, "The Murders in the Rue Morgue," was published in 1841, "The Mystery of Marie Rogêt" in 1842, and "The Purloined Letter" in 1844.

11. I discuss "The Mystery of Marie Rogêt" in more detail in chapter 4.

The common ground between Poe and Lovecraft where detective fiction is concerned is the idea of epistemological order and disorder (Cassuto 50). Epistemological order—that is, having an orderly understanding of how we know what we know—underpins social norms. Resolving epistemological disorder helps to restore social norms. Poe's tales of ratiocination, as with many detective fiction works, use the act of rational examination to restore epistemological order and social norms (Sayers 102; Landrum 52). This sense of order is a part of their popular attraction. After all, the comforts of middle-class life are enjoyed through the resolution of self-induced fear or tension. As Pittard notes, "the very structures of 'community' and 'family' are crucial to the construction of the criminal as a figure to be feared. Because these social units encourage and fetishise order, the appearance of disorder, no matter how localized, becomes a universal threat" (69–70). This engagement of disorder is central to Poe's story.

Poe's detective C. Auguste Dupin, as part of his personal investigation into Marie Rogêt's death, goes into significant detail discussing the various newspaper articles covering and updating the police investigation (Poe 175–78, 182, 192–93). This need to examine and to reveal is part of the process of restoring social and epistemological order; without it, the risk of more murders and more disorder is high. As René Girard notes in his work on early social groups, which I discuss in greater detail later in this chapter, at the core of social order is the need to suppress violence so that it is not replicated, and the figure who suppresses violence can be traced to the detective.

For his story about Marie Rogêt, Poe takes the true crime event of Mary Rogers's death in New York as the basis for his narrative (169). Dupin is socially prominent and thus at a social arm's length from both the reader and the police force representatives. This distance moves him closer to the fringe, as do his dalliances with decadence. His investigative procedures and mental processes are opaque at best (Sharp 65–66). The victim in Poe's story is a mere shopgirl who would have been otherwise unknown but for her exceptional beauty. Her existence itself is not a violation of the social order; Mlle. Rogêt's disappearance causes the first episode of epistemological disorder. When questioned, her aunt states that she has not seen Mlle. Rogêt, even though the girl told a male acquaintance that she was going to visit her aunt (173). The discovery of the girl's body in the Seine (174) throws Parisian society into full-blown epistemological disorder. Newspapers and their editors, all created by Poe but based on actual publications produced in New York during the Mary Rogers investigation, devote numerous column inches to speculation on methods and motives, and until Dupin becomes involved, the police suspect a gang of ruffians are responsible for Mlle. Rogêt's death. Dupin brings his considerable exegetic skills to the case and determines that a particular sailor is instead the one who is likely responsible for the girl's death (204–6).

Much of Dupin's exegesis is devoted to these newspaper accounts and editorial commentaries. Poe concludes the story without showing the arrest of the sailor, thus dismissing the importance of the revelation of the criminal, confirmation of the criminal's guilt, and denouement of the details of the case. Instead, the importance is the opportunity it provides Poe to lay out the structure of the detective fiction short story. Through footnotes inserted in the story text, Poe references the actual texts and events of Mary Rogers's death, illustrating his methodology. Like both a criminal and a detective, Poe reveals and explains his plot.

Despite these revelations, Poe's Parisians may never see a full return to normality. As Leonard Cassuto observes in his essay "Poe's Force of Disorder," "Dupin is Poe's agent for epistemological order. The sleuth's role in the detective stories is not so much to solve the crime as it is to save the entire category system, the reliability of which the crime has called into question" (50). The category system gives the investigation moral significance. For epistemological order to be restored, the criminal investigation must be on par with a scientific investigation, i.e., a truth-finding pursuit. It also must represent normative values so that it can attribute responsibility to the offender. Because of this risk imposed on the category system, detectives wrestle with moral issues as well as criminal ones (Poirier, "Ripples" 217). The nature of crime is such that it cannot be destroyed, only temporarily hidden. Crime transgresses boundaries by its very existence. If a central human desire for harmony and order exists, then crime violates that desire through its innate ugliness and disharmony.

A note here on the distinction between detective fiction and mysteries is appropriate. Larry Landrum, in his book *American Mystery and Detective Novels: A Reference Guide*[12] observes that

---

12. Landrum's *Guide* is a critically important reference work for students of detective fiction.

[d]etective stories are more specific than mysteries. They focus the narrative more directly on the solution of a puzzle than the solution of a crime poses. Detective stories demand keen observation, superior reasoning, and the disciplined imagination of their protagonists . . . . [d]etective novels as a more specialized form of the mystery are constructed around the formal investigation . . . while mysteries more broadly address the solution to a generally threatening situation. (ix–1)

In terms of interest to the detective, though, these boundaries are not hard and fast, as Doyle (through Watson) observes in "A Scandal in Bohemia." Waiting for Holmes to return home, Watson muses, "I was already deeply interested in his inquiry, for, though it was surrounded by none of the grim and strange features which were associated with the two crimes which I have already recorded, still, the nature of the case and the exalted station of his client gave it a character of its own" (14). Irene Adler's machinations are of as much interest to Holmes and Watson as are the crimes they recently investigated, even though Adler has not yet committed a crime against the King of Bavaria.

At first blush, it would seem that Lovecraft's stories are more mysteries than detective fiction, and they do indeed largely concern themselves with threatening situations. We may ask, then: did he write mysteries, or did he write detective fiction? Strictly speaking, he wrote weird fiction, so neither answer is correct. However, in his earlier stories, his narrators are out to solve mysteries, such as in "The Statement of Randolph Carter" (1919), which involves Carter and his companion Harley Warren trying to find a mysterious passage to the underworld (albeit in Florida, an unlikely locale). Lovecraft's later stories, especially "The Call of Cthulhu" and some stories published after it, have narrators who become investigative in their attempts to understand events, some of which involve crimes.

For Lovecraft, the thrills of Gothic horror and the broad devices of detective fiction are trappings, not substance, and are an unsteady structure for weird fiction. For instance, Lovecraft discusses numerous works by William Hope Hodgson in "Supernatural Horror in Literature," and his opinion of *Carnacki the Ghost-Finder* places that collection at the bottom of his list of Hodgson's works. For Lovecraft, the combination of a "conventional stock figure" with "an atmosphere of professional 'occultism'" is nearly fatal to the narrative (*CE* 2.115). Similarly, in his discussion of Algernon Blackwood, Lovecraft describes *John Science—*

Physician Extraordinary as "[m]arred only by traces of the popular and conventional detective-story atmosphere" (*CE* 2.121). Despite these traces, as well as the "professional occultism" in Blackwood's story "The Camp of the Dog," found in the above-referenced collection, Lovecraft notes that the stories are among Blackwood's best, producing "an illusion at once emphatic and lasting" (*CE* 2.121).

The elements of detective fiction in Lovecraft's own work go well beyond superficial application. In a letter to Alfred Galpin, Lovecraft states that he read all the published Sherlock Holmes stories as a boy (191). As Darrell Schweitzer notes in his study of Lovecraft and detective fiction, Lovecraft in his reading of pulp magazines would have read numerous detective stories in publications such as *Argosy* and *All-Story* (20). And although Schweitzer characterizes Lovecraft's maturation as a writer as involving "a philosophical parting of the ways" with detective fiction (21), Lovecraft does acknowledge Holmes's "brilliance and rationality and the deft artistry of the Doyle stories" (22). Of course, Lovecraft would not be attracted to crime alone, given his cosmicism, and Schweitzer notes this (22). But Lovecraft's lack of attraction goes beyond a mere rejection of the supernatural, as Schweitzer asserts (23). And although Schweitzer agrees that "many Lovecraft stories resemble detective stories in their structure" (23), more attention to Lovecraft's stories reveals that the structure allows Lovecraft first to invoke, then to invert the tropes of detective fiction. Schweitzer concludes by acknowledging that "[w]hat Lovecraft was doing, then, was applying the Holmesean method to the universe at large . . . his characters proceed with the same logical, step-by-step deduction that Holmes used for mundane matters" (24).

In his landmark two-book biography *I Am Providence: The Life and Times of H. P. Lovecraft,* S. T. Joshi adds details to the interplay of Lovecraft's works and detective fiction. Lovecraft was mindful of the market for detective fiction among readers of popular fiction. Joshi notes that in 1925 Lovecraft tried to sell "The Shunned House" to *Detective Tales* (592), but it was rejected. Later that year in August, Lovecraft spoke of writing a piece with a "detectivish" slant (592) but apparently did not. The same month, he spoke of sending "The Horror at Red Hook" to *Detective Tales,* given that its main character Malone is "a much more orthodox detective than any character in previous tales of Lovecraft's" (592). And in fact, Lovecraft submitted "The Call of Cthulhu" to *Mystery Stories* in the spring of 1927; it was rejected, not because the story didn't involve a mystery, but because it was "too heavy" (675). Even though Lovecraft did not write detective fiction per se, he favored the genre in some ways and used its elements in selected works.

Detective fiction itself has a teleological purpose related to society, just as Lovecraft used detective fiction elements in service of his larger cosmic views. In most detective fiction the revelation of the truth has a normalizing effect on the social order. Through investigation and revelation, the detective restores order where the criminal has caused disorder through his socially destructive actions. Lovecraft's fiction contains these elements as well, but in Lovecraft the impulse is described, then turned. Lovecraft establishes the idea of social order, then inverts it, using it as a tool to expose the horror at the core of cosmicism. Although in detective fiction the normative effect of the detective's actions enables the resolution of the case, this approach, this desire for epistemological order, cannot hold in Lovecraft. With figures such as Thurston in "The Call of Cthulhu," the investigation only seems to be a way to resolve matters: there can be no resolution for humanity in its encounters with cosmic horror.

The overall plot elements of "The Call of Cthulhu" are like those of garden-variety detective fiction, especially that published during the Golden Age,[13] but the critical difference is Lovecraft's cosmicism and cosmic horror. Whereas the detective in mainstream detective fiction focuses on a relatively limited scope of items and events, Lovecraft's investigators feel their awareness wrenched open by cosmic revelations. In Thurston's case, even the discovery of the cult in southern Louisiana was only a tease, an initial mundane experience leading to further investigation. The narrative of the Norwegian seaman Gustaf Johansen and his account of the rising of R'lyeh reveals to Thurston man's tenuous place in planetary history. As S. T. Joshi notes in *H. P. Lovecraft: The Decline of the West*, "What we are presented with in the tales beginning with 'The Call of Cthulhu' is a series of counter-civilisations—civilisations in many cases as fully evolved as our own but implacably hostile or at least carefully indifferent to ours" (338). At the end of the story, Thurston knows he will die at the hands of the cult, yet his certainty is diminished, perhaps only slightly, by his new understanding of the larger cosmic ends the cult seeks to realize. Thurston tells us that

---

13. The Golden Age of detective fiction occurred from roughly the 1930s through the first part of the 1950s and paralleled the appearance of the hard-boiled detective.

there was one box which I found exceedingly puzzling, and which I felt much averse from shewing to other eyes. . . . I succeeded in opening it, but when I did so seemed only to be confronted by a greater and more closely locked barrier. For what could be the meaning of the queer clay bas-relief and the disjoined jottings, ramblings, and cuttings which I found? (*CF* 2.382)

Ordering the contents of the box leads to Thurston's eventual comprehension of their significance, which is typically a normative function, and in mainstream detective fiction normative functions bring understanding and relief to the detective and to the community at large. However, the ordering of this box's contents begins an investigation that exposes Thurston to the experience of cosmic horror, which sets aside the normative functions of comprehension and understanding. Revelation leads to exposure and psychological damage, not resolution and restoration.

Thurston's discovery introduces epistemological disorder, i.e., the "greater and more closely locked barrier" to his understanding of the mysterious events. Rather than a physical barrier, Thurston experiences an inability to fully understand the significance of the items in the sealed box. The barrier is in his mind, and the more he discovers, the more disorder is revealed.

Epistemological disorder is one element introduced by the crime and the criminal, but it alone is not enough to power the plot of a given work of detective fiction. After all, a puzzle game stirs epistemological disorder until it is solved, and merely having certain elements in a plot is not sufficient to classify a literary work as detective fiction. And detective fiction is much more than a collection of signs and symbols. As Brooks Hefner notes in his article "Weird Investigations and Nativist Semiotics in H. P. Lovecraft and Dashiell Hammett," an "emphasis on semiotics appears in a variety of pulp genres, including both the weird tale and the detective story, each of which turns on questions of investigation and interpretation: in other words, the reading of signs" (656). Detective stories go far beyond the simple plot structure of crime, investigation, capture, and punishment. The genre of detective fiction has a tripartite dynamic at its core, that of the detective, the criminal, and society. This notion is derived from the work of sociologist René Girard on ritual violence and social order as necessary aspects of the sacred.

In his seminal work *Violence and the Sacred,* Girard discusses the critical relationship between ritual and sacrifice in early societies. As a sociologist, Girard is primarily interested in the social origins and consequences of ritual violence (4). The fear of violence is based on the fear of mimesis, i.e., the fear that violence once begun will spread uncontrollably. Mimesis, as a specific understanding of a sign or signs, is both cause and motivation for ritual violence: to prevent mimetic violence within a group, the priests of that group perform acts of violence on chosen victims. This ritualized violence is an act of community reconciliation (8) because the act of violence, when performed by a priest, cleanses and redeems the community. Because vengeance is a never-ending process, ritualized violence must be used to end it. And because all members of society are susceptible to the physiology of violence, all are affected by it. Girard observes that "[r]ecent studies suggest that the physiology of violence varies little from one individual to another, even from one culture to another. According to Anthony Storr, nothing resembles an angry cat or man so much as another angry cat or man" (2). Mimesis is independent of cultural variables, so the risk of the spread of violence is also independent of those variables. The "menace of chain reactions" (39) becomes the greatest risk.

The priest steps in as the mediator between the sacrifice and the community. The risk of the spread of violence can be abetted through ritual sacrifice, and accordingly, the priest sacrifices the victim in a ritual designed to bring the violence to an end (144). This sacrifice protects the community and restores peace by eliminating the source of violence, whether that source is the actual perpetrator or an agreed-upon scapegoat (42).

Given the mediating relationship of the priest to the community through the act of ritual violence, we can begin to see the relationship of the priest/sacrifice/community to that of the detective/criminal/society. The detective performs the parallel function of the priest by responding to the crime and discovering the identity of the murderer. The criminal, once at large but now identified (if not captured), must be sacrificed in a cultural context and manner that will redeem society. Should the criminal not be caught, the risk of mimetic violence increases. With each unsolved crime, that risk increases. It is critical that the detective catch, or at least identify, the criminal so that society is not increasingly implicated in its own violence. In the act of identifying and capturing the criminal, the detective restores the norms and stability needed for social functioning.

As part of a larger discussion of ritual violence in literature, Girard examines several Greek tragedies. He notes that the tragedy *Medea* "reminds us of a fundamental truth about violence: if left unappeased, violence will accumulate until it overflows its confines and floods the surrounding area. The role of sacrifice is to stem this rising tide of indiscriminate substitutions and redirect violence into 'proper' channels" (10). Similarly, the violence in *Oedipus the King* first raises Oedipus to the throne, then causes his downfall. Oedipus is both an investigator/priest and a criminal/sacrifice. His drive to discover the killer of Laius, his own father and the previous king of Thebes, leads to the revelation that he himself is the murderer. In this cultural context, Oedipus' banishment lifts the plague from Thebes, redeems the community, and restores the social order.

The threat at the core of *Medea* and *Oedipus the King*, the threat of violence and destruction, is the same threat recognized by Lovecraft's narrators. The alien, sometimes extradimensional creatures the narrators encounter pose an existential threat to human society. Sometimes the unfortunate narrator himself becomes the sacrifice in the tripartite dynamic, even if only a psychological sacrifice. As Peter Counter notes in his article "The Strange Game: When Sherlock Holmes Meets H. P. Lovecraft,"

> The detective, when placed in the tradition of cosmic horror, is heroic for holding on to humanity in the face of forbidden knowledge that which would drive weaker-willed individuals mad. They are the explorers and prospectors of existential frontiers, a testament to our unshakeable human condition. [They] are able to look into the darkness for meaning and upon finding the incomprehensible, accepting the challenge of living as a human in the abyss.

The consequence of being that "human in the abyss" is that the narrator lives in both worlds, in a sense—not fully in one because of his knowledge of the other. This parallels the detective's liminal state between the criminal world and society at large. As Pittard reminds us, if crime is "matter out of place," then the person investigating that crime is contaminated by that disorder (3). Similarly, as Peter Cannon notes in his article "Parallel Passages in 'The Adventure of the Copper Beeches' and 'The Picture in the House,'" "[A]n isolated environment can drive people, especially unenlightened ones cut off from the civilizing influence of the outside world, to commit horrible crimes with no fear or concern for the possible consequences" (5). Both Doyle's and Lovecraft's narrators are at risk of the consequences of too much knowledge. Instead of the Enlightenment ideal of broadening and deepening ourselves and our worlds, knowledge brings about isolation. Even Lovecraft's Great Old Ones in

Antarctica, the secondary protagonists of that tale, are brought down by their knowledge of the horrors in the old city.

Yet Lovecraft's narrators are not deterred by the prospect of disorder, whether personal or social. These men, and they are men, from various walks of life possess the curiosity, courage, and determination that are key to the development of investigative sensibilities. As Joshi notes in *H. P. Lovecraft: The Decline of the West,* Lovecraft observed that "the sensitive are always with us, and sometimes a curious streak of fancy invades an obscure corner of the very hardest head; so that no amount of rationalism, reform, or Freudian analysis can quite annul the thrill of the chimney-corner whisper or the lonely wood" (118; quoted from *Annotated* 25–26). Consider, for instance, Nathaniel Wingate Peaslee's determination to find the source of his dreams, and his harrowing trip through the Australian desert only to discover his own handwritten record in the archives of the Great Race. Similarly, in *At the Mountains of Madness,* William Dyer follows the history of the Great Old Ones through their icy Antarctic city, tracing figures in bas-reliefs lit by his and Danforth's flashlights and learning the scope and depth of the Old Ones' civilization. Dyer's scientific training helps him become, at first, a detective on the trail of the killers of his crew members. These killers, as quasi-criminals, then become victims of horrors much worse. The disturbing experiments on Dyer's crew—a matter of disorder that becomes understandable as Dyer learns more about the Old Ones, to the extent that he refers to them as "men"—shrinks in comparison to the horrors that wait for both Old Ones and humans in the Antarctic city.

In Girard, we have the priest/sacrifice/community. In detective fiction, we have the detective/criminal/society. And in Lovecraft, we have the narrator/cosmic horror/society. But these tripartite dynamics alone are not enough to energize a story. From these dynamics come the power for numerous tropes that energize both detective fiction and Lovecraft's weird fiction. A short list includes elements such as

- Tropes of vision: revelation/concealment, light/darkness, and clarity/obscurity, which Lovecraft uses deftly in the first paragraph of "The Statement of Randolph Carter" (1919) and in numerous other stories
- Masking/unmasking, most deliberately used in "The Whisperer in the Darkness"

- Sin/atonement, which is obliquely referenced in the earlier stories, usually matched with a character's twisted sense of aesthetics
- Private/public, seen in the raid on Innsmouth, a raid conducted in private and later made public, as well as any of the stories involving concealment of actual events[14]
- Guilt/confession, such as the opening of "The Thing on the Doorstep"
- Amateur/professional, most often seen in the contrast between the cop on the beat and the private eye; that most, but not all, of Lovecraft's narrators are amateurs at investigation
- Truth/deceit, where Lovecraft's narrators cannot reveal the truth without being accused of some form of deceit, including self-deceit
- And finally, the critically important trope of the palimpsest

In detective fiction, the umbrella trope is revelation and concealment. In its simplest form, where the detective reveals what the criminal has attempted to conceal, we find tropes of vision, identity, guilt, privacy, truth, and capability. Ideally, the detective reveals the truth by bringing to light clues and information about the crime, making clear what is important and unmasking the criminal. In early detective fiction, as well as later, in more mainstream detective works the criminal confesses his crime, and the entire story of the crime is made public to a degree suitable within the story's context. Darkness is dispelled, masks are discarded, and sins are atoned, and in the process the community is redeemed by having the criminal removed from its midst. Whether the detective is a professional or an amateur, all is resolved.

These dynamics are a critical aspect of Lovecraft's works, though employed to different ends. He uses, then subverts, the genre's conventions. In most detective fiction, a detective investigates a crime or mystery, then presents a clear-cut case with facts to support the conclusions. The offender is caught and justice is served. In contrast to these conventions, Lovecraft's investigators are sometimes unreliable, yet the reader comes to trust them during the course of a given narrative. Investigations lead to the dire clarity of cosmic horror, which must then be concealed. Truth and deceit are meaningless in the face of cosmic horror, yet that horror lends strange energy to the investigator's

---

14. The classic film noir *Chinatown,* which is also a work of detective fiction, uses this trope to heartbreaking effect.

pursuit of the truth. Evidence and facts are collected yet have uncertain status. Confessions are disregarded, crimes are concealed, and investigators face incarceration, while perpetrators cannot be caught. Justice cannot be served because no redemption is possible.

A clear example of Lovecraft's inversion of the revelation and concealment trope occurs when Dyer sets down his account of the Antarctic expedition, not to exhort the authorities to act, but to implore them not to (*CF* 3.11–12). Humanity cannot defeat the shoggoths inhabiting the Old Ones' city without facing mass insanity, and the knowledge of the Old Ones' history would be too disturbing for modern-day humans to accept. Should we learn that we were created as a species by the Old Ones as an experiment-turned-joke (*CF* 3.40), rather than by the hand of an omnipotent, omniscient deity, civilization and social order would be shattered. This trope of concealment for the good of society reaches back through numerous works by other authors. As Gavin Callaghan notes in his article "Elementary, My Dear Lovecraft: H. P. Lovecraft and Sherlock Holmes," "[M]uch like Lovecraft's Dyer and Danforth, who 'had to adopt an actual rule of strict censorship' in what they told, in the interest of 'the public's general peace of mind,' so too will Holmes and Watson conceal far more than they reveal with regard to events of both public importance and personal privacy" (226). Rather than revelation, Dyer begs for concealment, not for the protection of Danforth and himself but for the greater good of the social order.

Similarly, "The Dreams in the Witch House" (1932) offers many examples of these inverted tropes. Walter Gilman becomes the detective who is both victim and investigator. His dreams lead him to a better understanding of higher mathematics, but at the cost of his physical well-being and sanity. He becomes increasingly unreliable, yet because the reader accompanies him in his dreams, and because of his bent of mind as a mathematician, we see the truth in his experiences. The more Gilman investigates, the closer he comes to cosmic horror, until he finds himself at the attempted sacrifice of a child (*CF* 3.266–67). There is no evidence, no set of facts that Gilman can present about his dream-world activities; a confession would be useless because it could not be corroborated. Justice cannot be served because Keziah Mason and Brown Jenkin exist in extradimensional space. Learning the truth brings about no resolution. The only concrete evidence that the authorities can consider is the mystery of Gilman's death and the pile of human bones later found on the site of the Witch House (*CF* 3.273–74).

Other tropes are used more directly. Masking is perhaps most famously employed in "The Whisperer in Darkness" (1930), where Albert Wilmarth learns from Henry Akeley that Vermont is teeming with extraterrestrials. As evidence sent from Akeley mounts, Wilmarth becomes convinced that an investigation would be worthwhile. His interview with Akeley is nothing short of bizarre, and after he discovers the nature of the alien machines, he sees lying on a chair the mask and hands used by one of the Mi-Go to impersonate Akeley (*CF* 2.538). Rather than being unmasked by Wilmarth as in a conventional story, the Mi-Go eventually unmasks itself, unconcerned with any consequences that mankind can muster. This unmasking occurs without revelation; Wilmarth does not see the creature behind the mask, only the mask and hands themselves.

Like other tropes, the trope of the palimpsest runs throughout both detective fiction and Lovecraft's works. In its original definition, a palimpsest is a manuscript page, usually vellum, on which the original writing has been scraped off so that later writing can be done, but on which traces of the earlier writing remain. These traces can be perceived, even if only partially. Medieval monks reused parchment in this way, and traces of previous words and letters potentially affected translations and thus exegesis (Wikipedia). In detective fiction this idea becomes the layering of terrain, activity, time, and significance. For instance, in detective fiction, a crime scene has multiple layers when understood as a palimpsest:

- The original site before the crime
- The scene during the commission of the crime
- The scene between the commission of the crime and the discovery of the crime
- The discovery of the crime at the scene
- The arrival of the police to the scene
- The establishment of the official crime scene by the police, usually defined by tools such as yellow tape and tent cards
- The arrival of the detective to the scene
- The collection of evidence at the scene
- Potentially the return of the criminal to the scene

- Potentially the presentation by the detective of the solution to the crime at the scene itself

The palimpsest, both here and in medieval documents, functions both temporally and physically. That is, the physical space takes on significance through layers of meaning assigned over time. Whereas the crime scene may have been an otherwise unremarkable place, the conduct of first the crime, then the investigation, adds significance at each step. Pittard also notes the importance of the palimpsest to the genre:

> Referencing this idea of layering, the literary critic Tzvetan Todorov argues that the detective novel "contains not one but two stories: the story of the crime and the story of the investigation" . . . the distinction between the story and the plot [is that] "the story is what happened in life, the plot is the way the author presents it to us." The plot of the investigation forms the body of the detective story and it is read by the actual reader; this includes the story of the crime, as read by the detective. (23)

This is the core structure of the palimpsest as presented in detective fiction, and Lovecraft's use of science and cosmic horror brought new elements into the mix. In Lovecraft, the palimpsest melds itself within the "cosmic" aspect of cosmic horror. Earth itself has been the scene of rising and falling alien civilizations; no place is spared. R'lyeh waits to rise again; Y'ha-nthlei houses the Deep Ones below Devil's Reef; Elder Things once inhabited their city in the warm forests of Antarctica; and flying polyps, the creatures who pursued Peaslee, lived in the underground caverns of the Australian desert as recently as the 1930s. Each of these layers, and more from other stories, have been discovered by inquisitive and sometimes terrified investigators, and their respective significance reckoned accordingly.

Lovecraft even uses the idea of the palimpsest in spoken language. Delapore, the unfortunate main character of "The Rats in the Walls," devolves after learning the truth about his cannibalistic witch-cult forebears, to the extent that he speaks in languages that, layer by layer, recede backward in time: "archaic English, Middle English, Latin, Gaelic, and primitive ape-cries" (Joshi and Schultz 222). The sheer force of Delapore's family history overwrites him, as it were, a consequence of his determined investigation. The identity he believed was authentic is consumed by his family history; the man himself is lost but for his physical self.

In an interesting re-envisioning of the palimpsest idea, Peaslee in "The Shadow out of Time" (1934–35) discovers in his own modern-day time the existence of his handwriting from aeons ago, locked away in the archive of the Great Race (*CF* 3.450). Rather than finding traces of the Great Race's writing in his own time, Peaslee finds the opposite. Because he drops the evidence in his desperate escape from the underground tunnels in Australia (*CF* 3.448), he cannot prove that his experiences have been authentic. Instead, he retains the dreams and memories, isolated in what he has learned.

Detective fiction as a popular genre has its roots both in stories with ancient origins and in core impulses in early societies; the impulse to structure and order our world so that we are kept safe is a constant. Lovecraft's fiction takes the impulses of modern man, as passed through millennia from early societies to the present day, and reshapes them to address cosmicism and cosmic horror. Even as detective fiction presents the ongoing struggle to restore social norms in a chaotic, violent world, Lovecraft takes those structures and norms as tools to demonstrate the impossibility of any kind of permanent social order. Although it is not obvious that numerous links exist between Lovecraft's work and structures used in detective fiction, a close, informed examination shows that they are numerous and substantial. From here, we can now turn to Southern literature and examine the similarities between it and Lovecraft's fiction.

Chapter 6: The Weird within the Real: Common Territories in Lovecraft's Fiction and Southern Literature

> The past is never dead. It's not even past.
>
> —William Faulkner, *Requiem for a Nun*

> I have found that anything that comes out of the South is going to be grotesque by the Northern reader, unless it *is* grotesque, in which case it is going to be called realistic.
>
> —Flannery O'Connor, "Some Aspects of the Grotesque in Southern Fiction"

Weird fiction would not seem to have much in common with Southern literature, especially the Southern literature written during and just after H. P. Lovecraft's life. One example: Lovecraft famously argued that William Faulkner's story "A Rose for Emily" could not be considered weird fiction because, despite its bizarre events, the story was plausible and thus did not liberate the imagination (Joshi, *A Subtler Magick* 49). Weird fiction takes as its locale bizarre or unusual locales, extraordinary characters, and circumstances that stretch the imagination. Of the many things that may be said about Southern literature, the above would not be typical. Likely because of this apparent lack of common territory, literary critics do not offer much analysis of Lovecraft's weird fiction alongside Southern literature, which prevents us from understanding the commonalities shared by the two.[1]

The lack of published commentary is understandable. Lovecraft's devotion to New England would lead most scholars to look at other topics, while researchers in Southern literature have only recently concerned themselves with weird fiction. Given that Lovecraft's New England seems quite distant from the

---

1. This chapter was originally a paper presented at NecronomiCon Providence, August 2019.

South, not only in terms of miles but also in terms of culture, the barriers to research begin with the conceptual. Elements such as cultural divergences, images of conflict and war, and assumptions about the inhabitants of both New England and the South present obstacles. However, these barriers are not so high as they might initially seem.

Historically speaking, the South is defined by the well-worn grooves of slavery, oppression, and war. When we seek a more literary definition of the South, Jay Ellis offers useful beginning observations in an essay on Southern literature's characteristics when he notes that "Southern and Southern Gothic have been configured through a regular trope of 'below'" (xvii). Both geographically and ideologically, the South has been seen as a place of darkness and fear, viscerally rendered by Harriet Beecher Stowe's *Uncle Tom's Cabin,* in one example, where Uncle Tom's fate is determined by his sale down the Mississippi River to Simon Legree in New Orleans. However, the literature of the South has wider circumstances than just the United States—it involves the Caribbean, Africa, and Europe, from the Middle Passage of the slave trade, to the folktales of Scottish and Irish immigrants, to the literature of the settlers during and after the Age of Empire. It is helpful to keep in mind when drawing the various axes of Southern literature within and against American literature that Ralph Waldo Emerson, the critically important writer and philosopher of the nineteenth century, holds New England as a universal center. Emerson's famous transparent eyeball, a master trope in his canonical work *Nature,* sees the "ascendancy of Commerce" in the North over "Feudalism" in the South, with the implication during Emerson's time being the ascendance of an industrial North over a slave-borne South (Ellis xxiv).[2] Emerson's ascendant North is above the South below it, helping establish the trope of "below" and enabling it to play out in the works of the writers who come after him.

In addition to definitions rooted in geography, the South is defined in economic and mechanistic terms. Its agrarian economy, especially after the Civil

---

2. Given the sheer amount of work done on race in the South, much less race in Lovecraft, this project unfortunately does not allow the space for a full discussion of either. For race in Lovecraft, S. T. Joshi has done extensive work for years on the topic. A consultation of his catalogue would be profitable, such as his early work *H. P. Lovecraft: The Decline of the West* (1990), where Joshi confronts the topic squarely, as well as shorter commentary such as "Why Michel Houellebecq Is Wrong about Lovecraft's Racism."

War, could not compete with rising industrialism and westward expansion, and the South fell farther behind the rest of America. Edgar Allan Poe characterizes the South in terms that we would now think of as describing abjection—see works such as "The Fall of the House of Usher"—with this largely the result of the association of abjection with the grotesque, a critically important association that I will address later.

An important context for both Southern literature and Poe is the Gothic. Poe's "work demonstrates how [American] Gothic"—which has its differences from Southern Gothic, which has its differences from the grotesque—"was ideally suited to the emerging artistic and political consciousness of the region" (Walsh 23–24).[3] In Poe's work, as well as in the works of other Southern writers, we see what will eventually become the Southern Gothic used as a tool to deconstruct both the cultural narratives promoting the rational, progressive values held close by the North and the patriarchal, patrimonial values defended by the South. This use of the Gothic has been characterized as "a Gothic passage where what we would prefer to forget will not stay buried" (Ellis xxxiii). Just as the past is not the past, per Faulkner, Southern Gothic reflects the South's ongoing struggle with its identity and its history, "investigating madness, decay, and despair, and the continuing pressures of the past upon the present, particularly with respect to the lost ideals of a dispossessed Southern aristocracy and to the continuance of racial hostilities" (Marshall 3). Although these struggles have shifted to some degree during the past century, identity and history are still critical today to an understanding of Southern literature.

Crucial to Southern identity is what Eudora Welty called a "sense of place" (8), with writers steeping their stories in numerous tropes dependent on Southern history and culture and developing new ones along the way. Still, the geographic delineations were only an idea, a creation of custom and a notion of who belonged where that was bounded by that same historical struggle with identity and history, defining the South's inhabitants through race, caste, and class. Regardless of custom and notion, that identity was a fiction, real only so long as its unreality was accepted as authoritative. A real place and real people

---

3. A full study of the Gothic—even just American Gothic—would require more space than is available for this article. One good place to start is Allan Lloyd-Smith's *American Gothic Fiction: An Introduction*, as is Leslie Fiedler's *Love and Death in the American Novel* (New York: Stein & Day, 2nd ed. 1975).

were transcended by an unreal idea. This idea of an unreal place is equally critical to Lovecraft's geographies. Both Lovecraft and Southern writers create literary geographies that are nonexistent yet crucial to their larger messages. As Mitch Frye notes in his article "Astonishing Stories: Eudora Welty and the Weird Tale," "The South that we hold collectively in our minds is not—could not possibly be—a fixed or real place. It both exceeds and flattens place; it is a term of the imagination, the site of national fantasy" (75). The New England of Lovecraft's stories is equally a place of imagination and fantasy. Grounded within a rational, everyday New England is Lovecraft's territory of the weird, populated with alien beings, time travelers, cultists, and other horrors.

For some, this unreality becomes an obstacle to understanding both Lovecraft and Southern writers, defeating a basic grasp of their respective messages and provoking caricature by the unwilling and uninformed. Frye rightly observes that "empirical space is deformed in literary discourses that address the South through calculated caricature: representation via misrepresentation or anti-representation . . . critical terminology [in literary discourses] stages the discussion in . . . unreal cartographies" (76). Given the common territories of the weird found in both Lovecraft and Southern literature, these unreal cartographies become the basis for the authors' sense of place, a topic I discuss later in this chapter. Frye also notes that "often the operative narrative mode of 'southern regional fiction' . . . is not precisely realism but a mutant form that borrows provocatively from the speculative fiction genres of dystopia, fantasy, science fiction, and the weird tale" (76).[4] The paradox is that caricatures in both Lovecraft and Southern literature arise out of a necessary process for both Lovecraft and Southern writers, a process that strengthened and solidified many of the respective works.

Numerous Southern writers are known across languages and cultures. Arguably, the greatest of Southern writers to date is William Faulkner. The significance and effect of his presence in the Southern canon cannot be overstated. His Yoknapatawpha County is an example of an unreal cartography that has

---

4. Space does not permit an examination of these genres within Southern literature. For dystopia, Cormac McCarthy's *The Road* is recommended, and for the weird tale, Fred Chappell's *Dagon* is a reliable treat. Anne Rice's *Interview with a Vampire* is an urban fantasy, while science fiction is well represented by authors such as Samuel R. Delaney and Octavia E. Butler. Additionally, Afrofuturism is a relatively recent subgenre of science fiction that has numerous adherents.

taken a permanent place in the Southern canon, not the least reason being its immersion within the Southern Gothic.⁵ Allan Lloyd-Smith, in his study *American Gothic Fiction: An Introduction,* links Faulkner and Lovecraft through the Gothic:

> Faulkner is another profoundly Gothic writer also working out of a dispossessed region afflicted by loss of a grander history than its present condition. In Faulkner's southern Gothic the present can only be understood in terms of a working out of events from the past which emerge in uncanny interconnections and buried lineages, warped by the dark tangle of slavery and racial persecutions. . . . The vernacular of the New England locals, their ignorance and interrelationships, and the sense of family history shown [in Lovecraft's works] have "regional realist" parallels with Faulkner's ignorant but deeply embedded Southerners, similarly represented by a sophisticated informed consciousness beyond their own reach. (116–17)

Lloyd-Smith notes that Lovecraft and Faulkner share characters who use vernacular speech, who are ignorant, who have consanguineous relationships, who cling to their family history (and in some instances, regional history), and who inhabit haunted areas, lost plantations or family estates, forests, swamps, and defeated towns. The characters in both Faulkner and Lovecraft are bound by the past to the past, even as the present drags them into unknown and unwanted events.

In addition to the influence and use of the Southern Gothic, Faulkner has been cited as one of the most important writers of the Southern Renaissance, a movement started by a group of poets and literary critics at Vanderbilt known as The Fugitives after their eponymous publication. Eventually, these writers would become known as the Southern Agrarians, a group opposed to the post-World War I industrialization of the South who were galvanized by, because supremely annoyed by, the critic H. L. Mencken, whose essay "The Sahara of the Bozart" was highly critical of the South and its literary output and prospects (Mencken 157–68). Primarily, the Agrarians believed that industrialization stifled creativity, that leisure was necessary for the full exercise of creativity, and that a return

---

5. Another example of unreal cartography would be Zora Neale Hurston's Eatonville, Florida, from her novel *Their Eyes Were Watching God.* Too many examples of unreal cartography exist in both Southern and African-American literature to list here.

to an agrarian lifestyle would provide the kind of leisure needed. Although Lovecraft cannot be counted among the Agrarians, he does share opinions with them. In a letter to Robert H. Barlow from September 1933, he writes,

> As for the native rustic population and its psychological twists—it would seem, after all, that novelists like Faulkner and his school are essentially right about the decadence of the backwoods. It is probably true that the sounder and higher-grade American stock hastened to branch out in various adventurous ways, leaving the field of small-scale agriculture more and more to those feebler elements in whom repulsive abnormalities are most easily developed. That is one of the penalties of the machine age, which has broken up the relationship between the people and the soil and ruined the thrifty, sound-blooded agrarian element which flourished a century ago in all but a few parts of the country. Today, the hereditary small farmer is more and more in danger of slipping back from the yeoman status to the sordid condition of peasant or "poor white." It is so everywhere—my "Dunwich Horror" dealt with such a retrogressive region in Massachusetts, while the unpublished "Beyond the Wall of Sleep" (which you may remember—it's now in Hornig's hands) touched on a case in New York State. (*O Fortunate Floridian* 79)

Other common elements in Lovecraft's work and in Southern literature involve the pull of ties of blood, as in "The Shadow over Innsmouth" (1931); a lack of economic or social justice; conflict between loyalty to family and adherence to justice; the necessity for the concealment of motives; and the almost desperate concealment of the truth. Additional characteristics include entrapment and despair, which we see in numerous Lovecraft stories; flight and pursuit; the inescapability of the past in the present, dramatically represented in stories such as, again, "The Shadow over Innsmouth"; extreme pressure of racial hostilities, which brings "The Horror at Red Hook" (1925) to mind; and the notion of a lost mythos (Lloyd-Smith 61), which in Lovecraft surfaces as rediscovered ancient cults, a trope permeating his fiction. Within this lost mythos of cults, we find the growing awareness that what was believed impossible is in fact real (Lloyd-Smith 117); Christ-haunted people and places (O'Connor, "Some Aspects" 44), which in Lovecraft becomes past-haunted; the styled intensity of violence (Lloyd-Smith 118), with Lovecraft's violence often deftly deferred and revealed at the same time; and the individual's relationship to the official past of memorialized statuary (Lloyd-Smith 118), most notably represented in both the famous statuette of Cthulhu in Lovecraft's story "The Call of Cthulhu" (1926), which comes to represent a past that has not remained in the past, and in the images found by the Antarctic scientists in *At the Mountains of Madness* (1931).

Through encounters with the weird, Lovecraft's narrators come to realize that beliefs held by scientific experts, authority figures, and others with similar status have been invalidated. This loss of the continuity of belief ultimately leads to the feeling of cosmic horror. Similarly, Southern writers in the early and mid-twentieth century struggled with the loss of traditions long held and the rapid influx of modernity brought about by technologic advancement in the twentieth century, and for writers like Flannery O'Connor the grotesque was the best way to represent this sense of alienation and loss. Ultimately, the loss for both Southern writers and Lovecraft is linked to the loss of their respective forms of pre-industrial agrarianism.

This brings us back to the Southern Gothic. Certainly, there are aspects of Southern Gothic literature that find resonance in Lovecraft's work, but that is because they both contain elements derived from American Gothic, which in turns owes fealty to European Gothic. Note that Lovecraft doesn't use the term "Southern Gothic," given that it wasn't coined until 1935 by Ellen Glasgow in her *Saturday Review* essay "Heroes and Monsters." That same year, in a letter to C. L. Moore, Lovecraft states,

> Many people wonder why I don't exploit the traditional element of weirdness in the South—the brooding cypress swamps, the mouldering plantation-houses, the whispered negro lore, etc., etc. The fact is, however, that I can't feel the same deep, Gothic horror in any mild and genial region that I can in the rock-strewn, ice-bound, elm-shaded hillsides of my own New England. To me, whatever is *cold* is sinister, and whatever is warm is wholesome and life-giving . . . an echo, no doubt, of my own tropic-loving constitution. (47)

However tempting, though, we cannot limit Southern literature to Southern Gothic. Alan Spiegel, in his article "A Theory of the Grotesque in Southern Fiction," contrasts the elements of Southern literature with the Gothic, emphasizing that Southern literature focuses on normal, daylight settings of ordinary communal activity, people living within society in a normative manner, and the grotesque character as the reactionary, calling attention to the Establishment's failings (434–37). Because of, first, the reasons reviewed here; second, the sheer diversity of works set in various places in the South; and third, the caste, class, and social structures found therein, Southern literature diverts toward the grotesque more than the Gothic, despite the deep roots of Southern Gothic.

This connection to the grotesque becomes a connection to realism rather than to naturalism, as one might ordinarily expect. In addition to his parallels with Southern literature and the Agrarians, Lovecraft's emphasis on realism is one of his strongest connections to Southern literature. His affection for Enlightenment styling, values, and language—all highly realistic—is well established. As Spiegel observes, "the methods of the eighteenth-century novel . . . tended to cultivate the mimetic and the historical, the analytic and the normative. . . . The normative . . . [has] continued in our own time, in the work of the Southern writer" (433–34). Spiegel notes that the key differences between Southern literature and other American genres "involve far more than a setting; rather, they also involve technique, tone, mood, point of view—in short, a fundamentally different vision of life" (434). This different vision of life, based in similar adaptations of eighteenth-century stylings and expanded through the twentieth century into the present day, is the center of the common territory between Lovecraft and Southern literature: the realism that depends on the past for its energies.

Also critical to the common territory is the return of the repressed, as described by scholars in multiple fields and predicted by Freud. The return of the repressed in Lovecraft is the arrival or return of figures who are not repressed and who cannot be suppressed. That is the real horror in Lovecraft: the eroding codes of control. Lovecraft's sense of place is not merely the history of New England, but also a landscape with its own history that is both looming and uncontrollable. Along with the different vision of life and the return of the repressed is the common territory of the grotesque, the gatekeeper to unvarnished reality.

In Lovecraft, if one were inclined to psychoanalyze his work, the return of the repressed does not bring forth guilt, responsibility, or violence, as it does in other writers. There is rarely a conventional villain present in Lovecraft's works, and even those such as Wilbur Whateley are motivated by power derived from cosmic horror rather than conventionally evil motives. The violence in Lovecraft, if described at all, is often discovered after the return of the repressed, occluded by hints, or left off the page entirely and implied by such devices as the abrupt ending of a letter or diary entry.

The key to Lovecraft's realism is his skill with concealment of the most flagrant elements of violence and horror. Lovecraft reveals as he conceals, preserving mystery through uncertainty (Poirier, "Dynamics" 129). This use of the mysterious both contributes to and distances meaning. Similarly, in writing about how authors use mystery and meaning, O'Connor notes that

> if the writer believes that our life is and will remain essentially mysterious . . . then what he sees on the surface will be of interest to him only as he can go through it into an experience of mystery itself. His kind of fiction will always be pushing its own limits outward toward the limits of mystery, because for this kind of writer, the meaning of a story does not begin except at a depth where adequate motivation and adequate psychology and the various determinations have been exhausted. Such a writer will be interested in what we don't understand rather than in what we do. He will be interested in characters who are forced out to meet evil . . . and who act on a trust beyond themselves—whether they know very clearly what it is they act upon or not. (O'Connor, "Some Aspects" 41–42)

The term "mystery" is the key in O'Connor. In Lovecraft's fiction, mystery is frequently fatal in its pursuit and revelation and rarely resolved satisfactorily (Poirier, "Dynamics" 124). Nevertheless, one can easily see that Lovecraft is a writer "interested in what we don't understand rather than what we do" and whose work is "pushing its own limits outward."

This rejection of limits leads us back to the grotesque, a matter of no small interest to numerous writers, among them Mikhail Bakhtin, who placed the emphasis in the grotesque on both incompleteness and the human body (Donaldson 577). The grotesque rejects limits simply through its existence—the grotesque is a statement about limits placed on others by society, and its existence affirms both the social norm and the rejection of that norm. Grotesques live on the edges of society, metaphorically if not physically. This is certainly true in a story such as O'Connor's "Good Country People" (1955), in which figures a woman who is grotesque in body because she has a missing leg; in mind because she has a Ph.D. in philosophy, far beyond the educational achievements of others in her small Southern hometown; and in attitude because she changed her name from Joy to Hulga, rejecting the beauty and spirituality in her given name.

In Lovecraft, the body in question is frequently that of the alien, the intruder, the one who threatens the narrator in some way, and in "The Rats in the Walls" (1923), the body of Edward Norrys becomes grotesque both in its appearance and in its use as a kind of unholy communion material. For Bakhtin, the grotesque body pulls apart "the confines of the apparent (false) unity of the indisputable and the stable" (Donaldson 580) through its simultaneous rejection and affirmation of norms. The one who rejects and affirms norms has a place only on the periphery, alongside the grotesque.

The shift from the Gothic to the grotesque in both Lovecraft and Southern writers is a shift from the external to the internal. The grotesque is not merely physical: it is attitudinal, spiritual, emotional. It is both an aesthetic category of art and literature and an epistemology (Moghadam 88). To live as a grotesque is to understand the world through its distortions, not simply because the grotesque himself is distorted but because the community around him is shaped by its response to him. The grotesque is "flesh made metaphor" (Moghadam 76), an action more than a person. In terms of situations belonging to the grotesque, the grotesque can arise from the "sudden placing of familiar elements of reality in a peculiar and disturbing light" (Moghadam 80). The grotesque can thus result from some form of degradation: if physical, from deformities, physical defects, or distorted, ugly appearance; if mental, from psychiatric disorders, nervous breakdowns, insanity, or aggression.

The grotesque is not limited to characters, however. In his essay "On Placing the Grotesque," Nahid Moghadam points out that its fluidity means the grotesque can be used in numerous forms and genres (88). This idea dovetails with one of O'Connor's observations on the widespread use of the grotesque: "When we look at a good deal of serious modern fiction, and particularly Southern fiction, we find this quality above it that is generally described, in pejorative terms, as grotesque" (40). The grotesque is another bridge between the weird fiction of Lovecraft and the realism central to numerous Southern writers. As one researcher noted, "Rather than a sensationalist freak or horror show, grotesque literature cuts through the veil of civility, through decorum and oppressive normative fabrications to expose a harsh, confusing reality of contradictions, violence, and aberrations" (Bjerre). For some, the grotesque is a central character, such as Benjy Compson in Faulkner's *The Sound and the Fury* (1929), an intellectually challenged man who narrates sections of that novel. For others, the grotesque is a lesser character, as in O'Connor's story "A Good

Man Is Hard to Find" (1955), where several characters are arguably grotesques, though to different degrees. The grotesque is not limited by caste, class, and social expectations; instead, the grotesque exists along the edges, between persons, groups, towns, and social structures. Two short stories, one by O'Connor and one by Lovecraft, reveal the common territories toward which the grotesque points us.

O'Connor's 1965 short story "Everything That Rises Must Converge" shares tone and texture with weird fiction. Although it presents no monsters, it certainly presents the grotesque; the central character Julian is grotesque not in the way he looks but in the way he refuses to publicly accept the values of those around him, especially those of his mother, despite the fact that he inwardly shares her values. The story does not rely on fear or terror, yet the readers of O'Connor's time, whatever their origins, could have been moved to recognize the degree of emotional force required to strike Julian's mother dead at the end of the story. For this text, weird ritual and science fiction have been replaced by the destruction of a changing social order through the single action of a woman on the street of a small Southern town.

The story is simple enough. Julian, a recent university graduate in English, is compelled to accompany his mother every Wednesday night to her reducing class at the local YMCA. As do the other minutiae of his life, this weekly trip strains Julian's nerves; his mother's new hat, a purple and green monstrosity, is the first point of conflict in the story. Julian's self-pity and snobbishness prevents him from accepting his mother as she is, a woman whose values can be charitably described as in retrograde. It also prevents him from taking seriously her comments about her blood pressure.

As he and his mother board the city bus and ride the four stops to the YMCA, Julian's mood improves slightly when a well-dressed African-American man gets on the bus. Julian moves to sit by him, not because he is genuinely interested in the man, but because he knows his doing so will irritate his mother, who, as predicted, looks at Julian with reproach. At another stop, an African-American woman and her preschooler get on the bus and take seats directly across from Julian's mother. Both Julian and his mother realize within moments that the woman is wearing the same purple-and-green hat as Julian's mother. Julian cackles aloud at what he believes is his mother's loss of face, but soon her affect changes first into a smirk at the woman, then kindness toward the preschooler. Julian's mother praises the little boy both with her words and with a smile that O'Connor describes as a weapon: gracious because offered to an inferior. Julian's mother and the little boy play peekaboo while the boy's mother watches, fuming.

The next stop is the YMCA, and Julian, his mother, the woman, and the boy move to the street. In a gesture well known to those familiar with the pre-desegregation South, Julian's mother offers the little boy a shiny new penny. This enrages the boy's mother, who punches Julian's mother, knocking her to the sidewalk. As the woman stalks off with her child, Julian lashes out at his mother, telling her she got what she deserved. Sitting upright on the sidewalk, Julian's mother is immobile, struggling to speak, red and purple blotches on her face, and when she gets up with Julian's help, she walks only a little way before dropping her purse and falling to the pavement, dead from a stroke, her face purple and her eyes defocused. Julian cannot accept this unmooring of his life, and we leave him kneeling beside her on the sidewalk.

This story uses elements of the weird to move first toward the grotesque, then the abject, as described by Julia Kristeva in her book *Powers of Horror: An Essay on Abjection* (1982). For Kristeva, the abject is that which has been cast out through taboo. The abject is the forbidden that is still attractive, even though it is not acceptable to the group as a whole (1). The act of casting out a thing as taboo and the subsequent group acceptance of the taboo is what makes culture possible, because it introduces boundaries and limits (12–13). In Lovecraft, abjection works through human culture, which is in the symbolic (Lloyd-Smith 114). Human culture is an agreement among humans about how humans are and how they live; cultural variation can negate the symbolic if the differences between cultures are wide enough. The agreement—that is, the agreement we hold about human culture—is the symbolic, both represented and delineated by that which is taboo.

Creatures, cultists, objects, places, histories, and events are all within the real, to use Kristeva's term, when they introduce, participate in, represent, or otherwise indicate cosmic horror, i.e., they indicate worlds, experiences, and creatures outside the human and the natural world (Kristeva 3–4). The real is outside the symbolic; the symbolic defines itself by that which is taboo. Thus, cosmic horror is the collision of the human symbolic and the alien real. Humans see the reality of alien beings, worlds, and experiences; they feel cosmic horror; and their response is a sense of abjection. In Lovecraft and Kristeva both, abjection is the consequence of cosmic horror.

The events in "Everything That Rises" forces Julian's mother to see the reality behind the bride-like veil within which she lives, which is to say, seeing that her values are now taboo—values are changing in her culture, but she is ossified. Her beliefs and values, which for her constitute the symbolic, cannot withstand this encounter with the real, as represented by the woman's rage and attack. This collision between the real and the symbolic, that is, the collision between that which is outside Julian's mother's cultural beliefs and values (the real) versus that which is agreed upon as culture (the symbolic) collide, generating the grotesque. Julian's mother changes from being a stereotypical Southern woman clinging to the past to a crumbling, crippled figure, destroyed by a challenge to her beliefs.

But threats to beliefs are Lovecraft's bread and butter. Sean Elliot Martin, in his study of Lovecraft and the grotesque, noted that "[t]he stories [in which Lovecraft critiques institutions of physical sciences] are most often narrated by characters who suffer mentally due to the violation of assumptions based upon the institutions to which they attempt to adhere" (93). In other words, these characters experience abjection when the real of the institutions of physical sciences collide with the symbolic of the violations of the assumptions insisted upon by those institutions. This results in destabilization of the paradigm, with the characters first attempting to defend the paradigm, as William Dyer does in *At the Mountains of Madness,* then stretching their beliefs farther and farther in an attempt to understand and rationalize the evidence before them.

Through those threats to beliefs, Lovecraft brings the grotesque into other stories. In his story "The Picture in the House" (1920), Lovecraft describes rural New England as where "the dark elements of strength, solitude, grotesqueness, and ignorance combine to form the perfection of the hideous" (*CF* 1.206). The main character is something of a mystery; as with many other Lovecraft stories, we don't know his name, but we learn about him through his reactions to the dilapidated, antique-filled house into which he is driven by a storm. Once inside, he is attracted to a book, Pigafetta's *Regnum Congo,* which, as he looks through it, opens up time and again to Plate XII, a depiction of a cannibal butcher's shop (*CF* 1.210). The owner of the house comes downstairs and is genial and kind in his speech, though his manner is as antiquated as his home.

As the old man talks, leafing through the *Regnum Congo,* pausing with near reverence at Plate XII, the narrator realizes that the old man may have prolonged his own life by eating human flesh (*CF* 1.216). Spared from the potential danger of cannibalism by a bolt of lightning that destroys the house and apparently the old man, the narrator wakes up by the blackened ruins of the house.

In Lovecraft's story, the narrator's encounter with the grotesque old man is contextualized by its similarities with Southern literature. We see the significance of family, ties of blood, the necessity of concealing family truths from the community, and the complexity surrounding violations of family norms. A yeoman farmer becomes a poor white, the result of the lost relationship between people and the land; this loss of class and caste then becomes decadence as people and families grow isolated. Finally, we recognize the inescapability of the past in the present, as seen in the iconography in the *Regnum Congo.*

Stolen land and bartered bodies run through both Lovecraft's fiction and Southern fiction. In Lovecraft, humans have occupied the land that belonged to no one prior to the age of humanity and that was occupied by entities who brought structures, items, practices, and relics that now evoke cosmic horror in humans. The grotesque in Lovecraft—whether a character or a situation—exists to bear witness to human insignificance in the light of a universe without grace, reflecting the inhumanity that is the context of the human. It is not merely nonhuman; it is inhuman and grotesque. The grotesque in Lovecraft is refutational in nature; this mode presents simultaneously an image of man's feebleness and an understanding of the impossibility of his beliefs about humanity and the universe. In Southern literature, especially in O'Connor and Faulkner, we see the impossibility of the views of both the dominant Southern culture—that of the landed wealthy—and those of characters subject to the power of the dominant culture.

The common characteristics between Southern literature and Lovecraft's fiction find their way to the grotesque and the abstract as rendered through the effects of industrialism, modernity, and loss. At the end of many of Lovecraft's stories, as well as the end of numerous texts in Southern literature, the reader is left with the understanding of that loss. From here, we can now turn to *True Detective* and examine how all these elements can be brought together.

Chapter 7: *True Detective*, Lovecraft, and the Cult of the Yellow King

Some things you must always be unable to bear. Some things you must never stop refusing to bear. Injustice and outrage and dishonor and shame. No matter how young you are or how old you have got. Not for kudos and not for cash: your picture in the paper nor money in the bank either. Just refuse to bear them.

—William Faulkner, *Intruder in the Dust*

If climate scientists have concluded that, based on current trends and best-case scenarios, Chicago will soon feel like Baton Rouge, then what will Baton Rouge feel like?

—Richard Misrach and Kate Orff, *Petrochemical America*

Up to this point, we've examined the major structural elements of this study: Lovecraft, Chambers, detective fiction, Southern literature, and Thomas Ligotti. Take away any one of them, and the study is incomplete. What remains is the task of bringing these elements together. Again, the question to answer:

> Given Edgar Allan Poe, detective fiction, Southern literature and especially Southern Gothic and the grotesque, aesthetics, epistemology, Thomas Ligotti's sense of conspiracy, the art and craft of investigation, Ambrose Bierce, Robert W. Chambers, Carcosa and the King in Yellow (the book, the play, and the figure), tropes and figures and the weird, how is that that only H. P. Lovecraft can pull all these threads, and more, together? How is it that without H. P. Lovecraft, *True Detective* season 1 could not have existed?

Let's address this catalogue in as orderly a fashion as we may. *True Detective* provoked wide commentary and cultural interest upon the release of season 1. Writers on popular culture outlets committed time, effort, and bandwidth to analyzing and predicting the solution of the core mystery, but unfortunately, few looked farther than that. Websites such as Screen Rant, Medium, Looper, Vulture, YouTube, Reddit (of course), and numerous other outlets and publications busied themselves generating content.[1] Viewers obliged by leaving intricately reasoned comments. Even a number of scholarly books have been published about it (see, for example, Graham and Sparrow's *True Detective and Philosophy*; for the reader with a lot of spare time and who is interested in another take on the larger context, there's a Goodreads reading list included in the Works Cited at the end of this book). Much of this analysis and commentary concerned itself with cat-and-mouse, solve-it-before-the-detective calisthenics. Some of the commentary was perceptive in its grasp of the road signs that *True Detective* offered its viewers.

For my purposes, one especially important thread led to the art book *Petrochemical America* by Richard Misrach and Kate Orff, which I discuss briefly in chapter 1 and which is an important part of this chapter's work. *Petrochemical America* documents the effects of the petroleum industry on southern Louisiana and the nuances behind the despair and corruption the industry brings into communities. Its focus is on Cancer Alley, a 150-mile winding stretch of the Mississippi River between Baton Rouge and New Orleans where numerous petrochemical refineries are located. This is the primary locale for season 1 of *True Detective*, important here because from the industrial economy of Cancer Alley comes both the economic and political power enjoyed by select citizens of southern Louisiana (and, in *True Detective*, probably those citizens involved in the cult of the Yellow King) and the economic and political disadvantages suffered by most of the populace there. The victims in *Petrochemical America* are garden-variety, everyday, working-class people, much like those we see in *True Detective* who are the families and survivors of the cult.

Similarly, *Petrochemical America*, a photography book that is also a data-driven examination of the development and consequences of Cancer Alley in southern Louisiana, presents landscapes that are impossible for humans to inhabit safely. The authors show us a world where larger-than-life forces—in this case, petrochemical manufacturers—have imposed poisonous landscapes on the inhabitants. Those inhabitants cannot change their landscapes back without extreme effort—both political and financial—and that effort leads to conflict, disease, and death. They now inhabit a world changed by a seeping, poisonous presence, and they are equally changed by it.

---

1. I have spared cluttering the Works Cited list with URLs for these easily discovered websites.

Importantly, *Petrochemical America* also provides critical imagery for *True Detective*. The opening credits for each episode of season 1 use multiple images from the book, over which are laid, or within which interact, the main figures and important illustrative scenes from the episodes. The land and landscape of southern Louisiana are the backdrop of ruin, waste, and death. The landscape is tainted by the present and grayed by the past, haunted by the actions of the people who have possessed it. Possession of the land and landscape has poison and profit as its consequences. The land becomes an impossible site to inhabit, even as those living there are trapped by the economies of power and profit.

The consequences for the land and the people are profound: the industry wounds the land and water with persistent carcinogens, which are then transmitted into wildlife and people. Land values plummet as the coffers of the corporation swell, sending those not already sickened into desperate attempts to gain employment outside of their economically devastated communities. This wounding of the environment works its way up the social chain, corrupting residents, politicians, and people of all socioeconomic levels through their dependency on an economic base that destroys itself from within. As with addiction and other forms of dependence, the municipalities in Cancer Alley cannot rid themselves of the perpetrators yet cannot survive without them.

This wounded landscape that can neither die nor survive, caught between life and death, is the landscape of both Chambers's victims and the characters in season 1 of *True Detective*. In Chambers, the Play changes the lives of the characters who read it by changing their understanding of the nature of the world. What was once reality—the world most people agreed upon—now changes into an existence with Carcosa and the King lurking in the shadows, ever reminding the characters that they bear the mark of the King inside their psyches. There is no redemption for either the world or the characters. The landscape has become impossible.

The violations of the landscape perpetrated by the Play and embodied by the mental illness that overcomes the characters in Chambers and in *True Detective* is prefigured by Lovecraft's use of cosmic horror as a trope of woundedness, itself a trope used to describe the state of the enlightened ones within the unenlightened masses. Because certain sensitives such as artists have a deeper understanding of the weird, they serve as ambassadors of cosmic horror. This deeper understanding has a deleterious effect on them, driving them to extreme actions. Lovecraft uses woundedness to describe the plight of those who encounter cosmic horror in stories such as "The Unnamable" (1923), *At the Mountains of Madness* (1931), "The Dreams in the Witch House" (1932), and any number of other stories.

Other scholarly treatments of *True Detective* include areas such as media studies (Demaria), Buddhism (Janning), posthumanist landscapes (Matthews), the metaphysics of investigation (Sheehan and Alice), transcendence (Weech), and any number of other approaches. The significance of Thomas Ligotti's book *The Conspiracy against the Human Race* has been covered in chapter 3; here, I will briefly note its place in the continuity between Lovecraft and Ligotti.

Nowhere is the genus–species relationship between Ligotti and Lovecraft made clearer than in Ligotti's own description of his psychological priming before he encountered horror literature and eventually Lovecraft. In Matt Cardin's excellent discussion of the relationship between Ligotti and Lovecraft, Cardin provides numerous quotes from Ligotti on Lovecraft's significance to himself both personally and philosophically:

> The idea, as well as the emotional sensation, that human notions of value and meaning, even sense itself, are utterly fictitious . . . (Cardin 96)

> Not long before I began reading Lovecraft's stories, I experienced—in a state of panic, I should add—such a perspective, which has remained as the psychological and emotional backdrop of my life ever since. (Cardin 96)

> [I] found that the meaningless and menacing universe described in Lovecraft's stories corresponded very closely to the place I was living at that time, and ever since for that matter . . . (Cardin 96)

At the tender age of seventeen, Ligotti read Shirley Jackson's *The Haunting of Hill House,* then found Arthur Machen's *Tales of Horror and the Supernatural* in a drugstore (Cardin 96). A few months later, when reading *Tales of the Cthulhu Mythos,* Ligotti felt it "set off an explosive sense of identification" (Cardin 97). Ligotti felt that, finally, someone else had seen the universe in the same way he had—that human constructs about meaning and purpose are thin and febrile—and, oddly, this grasp of meaninglessness, this camaraderie, gave Ligotti a sense of purpose and a motivation to write (Cardin 98).

Ligotti hews close to Lovecraft in his descriptions of his own experiences

7: True Detective, Lovecraft, and the Cult of the Yellow King   117

during his spontaneous encounters with that intensely personal, immediate interpretation of cosmic horror. Cosmic meaninglessness follows cosmic horror closely, as Lovecraft showed us. But Ligotti's experience and subsequent writing career follow a long and proud legacy that apexes in *True Detective:* Chambers first conjured the world of the Yellow King; Lovecraft took what pieces he found useful and brought them into his stories; and Ligotti united Lovecraft's cosmic horror with his interpretation of Schopenhauer's pessimism to craft his own pessimistic worldview, later to be incorporated into Rust Cohle's personal philosophy in *True Detective*.

This spine running from Chambers to Lovecraft to Ligotti to *True Detective* both illustrates the structure of the legacy and demonstrates how critical Lovecraft's role is in it. Chambers's *King in Yellow* provides a mythic framework for the plot; but without Lovecraft's intense, emotionally immersive presentation of the individual's confrontation with cosmic horror, Ligotti would not have found the reflection of his own cosmic horror crisis and, quite possibly, if he had developed his philosophy of pessimism at all, would probably have done so along a different path.

This argument may seem to ignore the necessity of Chambers and Ligotti in this intellectual atmosphere, and indeed, without Chambers this particular mythic structure evaporates. Chambers's absence would require Nic Pizzolatto to find a different mythic structure around which to build his story, but one could argue that there are plenty of those.

Ligotti's absence from the intellectual atmosphere would result in a pessimism perhaps less intensely personal in Rust Cohle, but one must remember that Ligotti's pessimism is part of a continuum—he's nowhere near the only twentieth-century pessimist—and dropping Ligotti out would only mean that Pizzolatto would need to find another source for pessimism. Perhaps Zapffe could have provided a similar role, given Zapffe's reliance on Schopenhauer and others.

But no Lovecraft? No keystone to the arch?

Without this literary Copernicus (as described by Fritz Leiber), without the thinker constructing and recentering the weird fiction universe in which mankind's insignificance cannot be rectified: a universe in which the pessimism Rust Cohle exhibits is not only rational but is the only reasonable response—not rational about the idea of human consciousness being a ghost inhabiting a puppet, but rational about the realization that humans are momentary, transient, and ineffective; that police work such as that done by Cohle and Hart means nothing once one looks outside the tiny, fragmented, limited, earth-bound view of humans; that human belief in ideas about goodness, worth, and value are temporary historical fictions—in other words, without Lovecraft's careful, precise, considered understanding of the truths behind human existence, *True Detective* cannot lay out its modern-day examination of where we stand.

With the line from Chambers to Lovecraft to Ligotti to *True Detective* established both here and in chapter 4, we can now turn to *True Detective*, Lovecraft, and the cult of the Yellow King. Season 1 of *True Detective* takes place in three time periods: 1995, when the murder of Dora Lange occurs and when Rust Cohle and Marty Hart initiate (and theoretically complete) an investigation; 2002, when new evidence about the activities of the cult of the Yellow King appears; and 2012, when Cohle and Hart, now both off the Louisiana State Police, finally confront the murderer after an even more intensive, albeit private, investigation. The action takes place in southern Louisiana, in towns along U.S. Interstate 10 for the most part, with one notable sequence, a botched robbery and shootout with a biker gang Cohle has infiltrated, taking place in east Texas (S1E4, "Who Goes There").[2]

During these three timelines, Cohle and Hart are forced to reckon with numerous difficult events: their growing recognition of their own personal failings, the disintegration of their professional relationship, their fragmented and unsatisfying love relationships, their individual rock bottoms. They are haunted by their own pasts even as they struggle with the investigation into the cult's activities and membership. These struggles remind any reader conversant in twentieth-century detective fiction—even if only through film and television figures—that the detective is both a semi-savior of society and a damaged criminal element. It's not possible for the detective to be one or the other anymore.

The larger cultural context for *True Detective* is a kaleidoscope of both the weird and the investigative, knit together by the theme of the haunted land-

---

2. Given the wide coverage of *True Detective* by online media and pop culture outlets, a full summary of the series would be redundant. Recommended online sources include Wikipedia for a conventional, TV-digest-style series of episode recaps; heavy.com for a briefer yet still informative take; and vulture.com for longer episode recaps with breezy yet insightful commentary.

scape. Chambers and Lovecraft are the literary aspects; Ligotti's contributions to Rust Cohle's personal philosophy and ultimate crisis of self are well documented; and Southern literature, especially but not exclusively Southern Gothic, is the wider context for Chambers, Lovecraft, Ligotti, and detective fiction. From Southern literature sprang the Southern Gothic, which is perhaps how the South is best known today, as discussed in chapter 6. The global imaginary holds the Southern Gothic as the "real South," a too-easy reply for a complex, rich, diverse, and historically burdened region. Nevertheless, this particular view of the South is the South of *True Detective*'s characters, a vista ranging from the deeply religious, to the grotesque, to the psychopathic. In short, the cohesion among these four elements—Chambers, Lovecraft, Ligotti, and detective fiction—would be difficult, if not impossible, without the presence of Southern literature and its subtheme of the haunted landscape.

As I discussed in chapter 6, the significance of the grotesque to Southern literature in general and *True Detective* in particular is key to understanding the broader social and cultural dynamics that Cohle and Hart move within. Cohle and Hart live within the degeneration of the ideal into the grotesque. Cohle's family life disintegrates, destroyed by the accident that claimed the life of his little girl; then he evolves into his lone-wolf-philosopher identity, rooted in Ligotti's pessimism and ticking down time until his own end arrives. In contrast yet nevertheless converging with Cohle, Hart's family life, destroyed by his casual infidelities, changes into a kind of lone-wolf existence as he becomes a private investigator after his retirement from the Louisiana State Police in 2006. Both men are haunted by their pasts, unable to wrest themselves away from what destroyed them. They live within the haunted landscape of the convergence of their personal histories with the larger history of southern Louisiana.

This contrast-into-convergence is characteristic of how some Southern writers dealt with the changing social codes of the twentieth-century South. Wrestling with the legacy of the past and uneasy about an economically destabilized future, Southerners and Southern writers attempted to make sense of the world—a new, and in some instances unwanted, world.

Faulkner's observation that "[t]he past is never dead. It's not even the past" (85) offers a bridge between the Southern literature of the late nineteenth and early twentieth centuries—that of what is essentially pre-modern Southern literature—and Cohle's now-famous, oft-quoted speech:

Why should I live in history? Fuck, I don't want to know anything anymore. This is a world where nothing is solved. You know, someone once told me time is a flat circle. Everything we've ever done, or will do, we're gonna do over and over and over again. And that little boy and that little girl, they're gonna be in that room again. And again. And again. Forever. (S1E5)

For many viewers of *True Detective,* this speech was the core of season 1, and for purposes of this study it is also the crossroads where Chambers, Lovecraft, Ligotti, and Southern literature meet. With regard to Chambers and Carcosa, a world where nothing is solved would be the kind of world suffering from an incursion of Carcosa: destabilized, uncontrollable, very nearly unreal, as we see the world inhabited by Hildred Castaigne. It is a world where madness cannot be conclusively fought, where norms are dismissed and replaced by a dreamlike unreality, and where misrule triumphs over the efforts of individuals to adhere to what is right, as we see in *Impossible Landscapes* and in Robin Laws's books *New Tales* and *The Missing.*

This is the world in which Hildred Castaigne lives, the layer of the palimpsest simmering underneath the reality that Castaigne's nephew Louis inhabits, the layer ostensibly under our own world. This is a human history without notions of meaning or significance. For Lovecraft, the meaninglessness of human conceptions of history and time is a core aspect of his weird fiction, so the ease of its use in *True Detective* is a given. Ligotti's philosophy as the core of Cohle's own philosophy is more complex, and I examine it in greater detail in chapter 3. The pessimistic tradition in Ligotti and his philosophical predecessors is well represented in Southern literature in various ways, from the near-fatalism that leads to class conflict in Faulkner, to the struggle against constraints in Flannery O'Connor, to the sense of inevitability in Fred Chappell's *Dagon.*[3]

All these positions are epistemologies; that is, they are attempts to describe the world in a way that makes it more comprehensible. They are attempts to develop a schema upon which meaning can be hung. They are ways of knowing how we know things, and in *True Detective* they are the ways that Cohle and Hart understand both the world and, within their respective worlds, the clues

---

3. Given that a book-length discussion could be devoted entirely to *Dagon,* I am not examining it here. I urge readers to pick it up, if for no other reason than to experience Chappell's excellent treatment of both the way a cult would operate in reality— no flowing robes, no wild, torch-lit dances—and the mind of a cultist going insane.

around the murders. One of the consistent characteristics of Cohle and Hart's relationship is that they represent battling epistemologies. Cohle's pessimism doesn't complement Hart's self-centered smugness so much as it fences with it, feinting and parrying the assumptions that Hart built into his comfortable, conventional, yet stultifying life. Hart is certain about his moral stances, which are those of the dutiful police investigator and the conventionally philandering husband. These walled-in certainties about life and ethics force an apostate like Cohle to explain and illuminate his positionality against conservative white Southern culture and norms.

These positions serve Cohle and Hart well—Cohle gets to feel smug about being brilliant in the middle of south Louisiana, Hart gets to feel smug as he watches Cohle's disintegration while ignoring his own wrecked life—yet both men are haunted by their histories and decisions. Cohle is haunted not only by his little girl's death, but also by his past police work and his failed marriage. His work as an undercover detective led to his abuse of drugs and, later, his stay in a psychiatric hospital; one consequence of these events is his experiencing sudden bouts of hallucinations, none harmful, yet their significance is ambivalent. As with other narrative elements we see in *True Detective,* they may be secondary, tertiary, or even more distantly connected to the central case, yet their visual qualities are haunting, and they draw the viewer and Cohle back into both the Dora Lange case and the nimbus of the Yellow King.

Unlike Cohle, Hart is haunted exclusively by the emotional fallout from his own actions, most prominently his numerous infidelities. Hart's conventional, superficially calm life is a cover for his taste for pretty yet vulnerable women in their twenties. He tries to be the solid, dependable, middle-aged white Southern male—family man, churchgoer, steady provider—but he is haunted by both the boredom of his life and the guilt of his secrets. But because Hart is no psychopath, he cannot wave away the emotional consequences of his infidelities. Instead, he is forced to carry them inside himself, a ghost in his own shell, deceiving others about himself and his actions—as if those deceits would matter in Ligotti's epistemology—and thereby playing out Ligotti's theory of humans being puppets inhabited by ghosts.

Cohle and Hart's battling epistemologies come to a head during the 2002 timeline of *True Detective*. Cohle has long been aware of Hart's infidelities, and Hart has been worn thin by Cohle's cold intellectualism and extreme rationality. After Cohle and Hart's mutual resentments erupt into a fistfight in the parking lot of a district outpost of the Louisiana state police, Cohle is kicked off the force and out of everyone's life (S1E6). Unfortunately for both men, things cannot improve simply by Cohle's removal from the scene. Both men will have to reckon with each other's epistemology: Cohle will have to face the critical human need for hope, something Ligotti remains adrift without, and Hart will have to make amends for his own darkness, something Ligotti would perhaps wave away as unnecessary.

Just as Cohle and Hart battle each other with their respective epistemologies, the Cult of the Yellow King uses the dark aspects of Southern history and culture against Cohle and Hart's attempts to investigate the cult and reveal its existence. This latter struggle of culture-within-culture is balanced on a fulcrum of power and violence, two of the core elements of Southern culture. Because Southern culture has slavery, Jim Crow, and oppression as its historical armature—much of it still minimized, altered, or denied and thus unresolved—it is impossible for Southern culture be other than as it is today. Without the open recognition of how denial still functions to serve power in the South, it is simply not possible for Southern culture to be any less violent; any less obsessed with history, genealogy, and family; and any less determined to cling to overt and covert structures of power. The history of Southern culture is bloated with incidents of the misuse of power and the stories of the oppressed. Because these factors are in place in reality, we find them reflected in *True Detective*. Within the cult of the Yellow King, the bare, terrible use of power and violence form the core of the cult's hold over its child victims. Again, it is impossible to have Southern culture and society constituted as it is in *True Detective* without a historical armature of power and violence; the fact that the cult uses similar structures in its practices is inevitable. Any horror that the viewer experiences as these structures are revealed must be recognized to be part of the supporting epistemologies for that power structure.

The proclivity for violence in Southern culture is so widely documented, so much a part of stereotypes about Southerners, that a mounted defense of the point seems unnecessary. What is interesting is how this armature of violence has some parallels in Lovecraft's fiction, even as it is teased out in *True Detective*. In Lovecraft, one of the inevitable consequences of human existence is the probability of human life coming to a violent end after the return of one or another alien entities or the arrival of an entity yet undreamt of by artists, poets, and seers. Not all alien entities are as amenable as the creatures in "The Whisperer in Darkness"[4] (1930), and not many alien entities seem to have the spirit of scientific inquiry that the Elder Things in Antarctica possessed, a spirit suffered by the dogs and men the Elder Things dissected. Entities such as Cthulhu have their own plans and barely notice human existence. The implicit, anticipated violence that is at the core of aliens' existence is a direct threat to human existence. This implicit, anticipated violence—the sense that a violent encounter is inevitable—is as much a part of Southern culture as it is in Lovecraft's stories, and we see a similar anticipation in *True Detective*.

However, *True Detective* comes at the violence in Southern culture from a different perspective. The threat, possibility, and past examples of violence are simply a norm within the cultural landscape, a norm surprising only to outsiders. Relationships between men in both Southern literature and *True Detective* are based in part on the expectation of eventual violence. As discussed in chapter 5 in the section on René Girard, ritual violence occurs to prevent outbreaks of future, uncontrollable violence. A fistfight between friends is one of those ritualized forms of violence that is intended to clear the air, somehow—to render something tangible or physical that has previously been emotional, unspoken, and intangible. Possibly it is an evocation of ritualized violence to enable and reconcile a taboo encounter of physical contact between males. When the atmosphere between Cohle and Hart becomes increasingly tense, we know that a fight is going to happen. They will fight not *in spite of* being educated, accomplished, and honorable men, but *because* they are.

At the same time, Cohle and Hart are so different that it is almost inevitable that they will fight each other; the fact that it takes place in the parking lot of the district office of the Louisiana State Police only underlines the ritual nature of the event. Hart's shooting of Reggie LeDoux while LeDoux was handcuffed is more than just revenge: it is an effort to re-establish power. Hart's beating of the two teenage boys caught with his daughter—done with the cooperation of fellow law enforcement officers—is similarly an effort to re-establish power. This violence parallels the violence in the past that has been

---

4. Unless one consults the numerous German Shepherd dogs that the creatures killed around Henry Akeley's Vermont home, that is. Cats tended to fare much better in Lovecraft's stories.

associated with the cult of the Yellow King as it exists within its larger, equally violent Southern culture.

These battles can be other than philosophical, of course. They are not limited to epistemology (though one could argue that they ultimately always are). One of the elements of detective fiction is the idea of battling narratives, that is, the battle between the narrative of the detective and that of the criminal. The detective recreates the crime narrative in an effort to eventually master it and thus master the criminal. In response to the detective's narrative work and in an effort to avoid capture, the criminal constructs a counternarrative, almost always false, that exculpates himself. The detective triumphs in part by recognizing the flawed narrative and superimposing the correct one over it. In much detective fiction, especially that before the middle of the twentieth century, this is sufficient to restore the norms of society and intervene with the criminal. However, in *True Detective* all these norms battle one another—the detectives versus the cult, the non-cult criminals versus the detectives, the cult versus normative society, the detectives versus normative society—in a landscape haunted by history and a culture haunted by violence, making impossible the restoration of norms other than those based in violence. It is the norms themselves that support the murders, the violence, and the corruption, and as such, the norms of middle-class American culture are undermined. In some ways this too is an impossible landscape, a thin veil of ostensible social norms concealing-while-revealing the true norms of power, violence, and corruption. As in Lovecraft and in Southern literature and culture, these norms have inevitable consequences for the people who live among them.

One of the things that makes this inevitable is the realism of the grotesque in Southern literature and the literary realism employed by Lovecraft, as he has noted and as I have discussed in chapter 6 (*CE* 2.177). In other words, the real is the ground of the weird, an essential context for our understanding of the weird. And although current subgenres of Southern literature explore possibilities beyond realism, it is the realism of writers such as Faulkner, O'Connor, Welty, Williams, and many others that provides the ground for the new subgenres we see today.

Yet here we must return again to the idea of the haunted landscape. All these writers are haunted in some way: Chambers is haunted by these early ideas of the weird; Lovecraft is haunted by a planetary landscape that is haunted by a past inhabited by aliens, a future haunted by the inevitable destruction of and loss of human civilization, and its eclipse by other, alien civilizations; and Ligotti (and later *True Detective*) is haunted by a landscape that is overdetermined by its inherited burden of history.

In this construction, the past cannot be the past. It must be the present and the future. Rust Cohle's "time is a flat circle" statement defines time with hard edges: if Cohle and Hart cannot intercede, the victims of the Yellow King will be doomed to yet another cycle of victimization and anguish. But will it be enough? Can the circle of time be stopped?

For Chambers and Lovecraft, the future holds not promise but change and death—the suicide portals in Chambers, mentioned multiple times by Hildred Castaigne in "The Repairer of Reputations," and the loss of humanity regardless of its efforts in Lovecraft. For Ligotti, human existence is on such uncertain terms that it is irrelevant whether the future holds anything or not, because humans can't tell if that future is possible when they can't even tell if the present is real or not.

Where, then, are we left? If Ligotti is correct about the haunting but got the locus wrong—if what we are is humans inhabiting a landscape, haunted by a past that isn't dead and isn't even the past, then how do we reckon with it? Once again, we can take Rust Cohle's advice: in S1E3, Rust tells Marty, "The world needs bad men. We keep the other bad men from the door," and in E8, as he has begun to convalesce both emotionally and physically, he tells Marty, "If you ask me, light's winning." We must accept that, far from being creatures of light and goodness, we humans are creatures of shadow and flaw, ready to be distracted by the ghosts in the landscape yet able to focus on the light and know it for what it is. It is necessary that we be the bad men sometimes so that the light can win.

Appendix:
True Detective Season 1 Cast

Creator/writer: Nic Pizzolatto
Director: Cary Joji Fukunaga
Televised on HBO: Episode 1 (12 January 2014); Episode 2 (19 January 2014); Episode 3 (26 January 2014); Episode 4 (9 February 2014); Episode 5 (16 February 2014); Episode 6: 23 February 2014); Episode 7 (2 March 2014); Episode 8 (9 March 2014).

Primary Cast Members

Actor	Role
Matthew McConaughey	Detective Rustin "Rust" Cohle
Woody Harrelson	Detective Martin "Marty" Hart
Michelle Monaghan	Maggie Hart (née Hebert)
Michael Potts	Detective Maynard Gilbough
Tory Kittles	Detective Thomas Papania

Recurring Cast Members

Actor	Role
Alexandra Daddario	Lisa Tragnetti, a court stenographer with whom Hart has an affair
Shea Whigham	Joel Theriot, a traveling minister
Jay O. Sanders	Billy Lee Tuttle, an influential reverend
Charles Halford	Reggie Ledoux, a drug producer
Glenn Fleshler	Errol Childress, a groundskeeper at one of Tuttle's academies
Joseph Sikora	Ginger, a gang member who has ties to Cohle
Lili Simmons	Beth, a young prostitute who knew Dora Lange

Brad Carter	Charlie Lange, Dora Lange's convict ex-husband
Kevin Dunn	Major Ken Quesada, Hart and Cohle's superior in 1995
Michael Harney	Steve Geraci, Hart and Cohle's colleague, later sheriff of Iberia Parish
Elizabeth Reaser	Laurie Perkins, a woman with whom Cohle becomes involved
J. D. Evermore	Detective Bobby Lutz, Hart and Cohle's colleague
Don Yesso	Commander Speece, Hart and Cohle's superior
Paul Ben-Victor	Major Leroy Salter, Hart and Cohle's superior in 2002

Works Cited

Anderson, James Arthur. *Out of the Shadows: A Structuralist Approach to Understanding the Fiction of H. P. Lovecraft*. San Bernardino, CA: Borgo Press, 2011.

Beginning with Buddhism. Tr. Thomas Byrom. Bigviewbuddhism. org/the-dhammapada-old-age.

Bjerre, Thomas Ærvold. "Southern Gothic Literature." *Oxford Research Encyclopedia of Literature*. DOI:10.1093/acrefore/9780190201098.013.304.

Bradshaw, Kathy. "Courir de Mardi Gras a Far Cry from Bourbon Street Antics." *The Advertiser* (26 February 2019). theadvertiser.com/story/news/2019/02/26/saddle-tramp-riders-traditional-cajun-courir-de-mardi-gras-lafayette/2983376002/.

Budden, Gary. "Awake Awake Sweet England: Why We Need Landscape Punk." thequietus.com/articles/23446-landscape-punk-nationalism-politics.

Buddha Dharma Education Association. *The Dhammapada*. Chapter 11, "Old Age." Verse 147. www.buddhanet.net.

Burleson, Donald R. *Lovecraft: Disturbing the Universe*. Lexington: University Press of Kentucky, 1990.

Callaghan, Gavin. "Elementary, My Dear Lovecraft: H. P. Lovecraft and Sherlock Holmes." *Lovecraft Annual* No. 6 (2012): 199–229.

Cardin, Matt. "The Master's Eyes Shining with Secrets: H. P. Lovecraft's Influence on Thomas Ligotti." *Lovecraft Annual* No. 1 (2007): 94–125.

Cassuto, Leonard. "Poe's Force of Disorder: The Grotesque in Cultural Context." In *Masques, Mysteries, and Mastodons: A Poe Miscellany,* ed. Benjamin F. Fisher. Baltimore: Edgar Allan Poe Society, 2006. 45–62.

Chambers, Robert W. *The King in Yellow and Other Horrors*. Ed. M. Grant Kellermeyer. Fort Wayne, IN: Oldstyle Tales Press, 2016.

———. *The King in Yellow: Annotated Edition*. Ed. Kenneth Hite. Chelsea, AL: Arc Dream Publishing, 2019.

———. *The Yellow Sign and Other Stories: The Complete Weird Tales of Robert W. Chambers.* Ed. S. T. Joshi. Oakland, CA: Chaosium, 2000.

Counter, Peter. "The Strange Game: When Sherlock Holmes Meets H. P. Lovecraft." *Everything Is Scary* (13 July 2015). www.everythingisscary.com/page/sherlock-holmes-meets-hp-lovecraft.

Demaria, Cristina. "*True Detective* Stories: Media Textuality and the Anthology Format Between Remediation and Transmedia Narratives." *Between* 4, No. 8 (November 2014): 1–25.

Detwiller, Dennis. *Impossible Landscapes.* Chelsea, AL: Arc Dream Publishing, 2021.

Donaldson, Susan V. "Making a Spectacle: Welty, Faulkner, and Southern Gothic." *Mississippi Quarterly* 5, No. 4 (Fall 1997): 567–84.

Doyle, Arthur Conan. "A Scandal in Bohemia." 1891. In *The Classic Illustrated Sherlock Holmes.* Stamford, CT: Longmeadow Press, 1987. 11–25.

———"The Man with the Twisted Lip." 1891. In *The Classic Illustrated Sherlock Holmes.* Stamford, CT: Longmeadow Press, 1987. 80–94.

Ellis, Jay. "On Southern Gothic Literature." In *Critical Insights: Southern Gothic Literature,* ed. Jay Ellis. Ipswich, MA: Salem Press, 2013. xvi–xxxiv.

Elmore, Rick. "Loving Rust's Pessimism: Rationalism and Emotion in *True Detective.*" In *True Detective and Philosophy: A Deeper Kind of Darkness,* ed. Jacob Graham and Tom Sparrow. Oxford: John Wiley & Sons, 2018. 31–40.

———. "The Secret Fate of All Pessimism: Time, Determinism, and Eternal Recurrence in *True Detective* Season One." In *True Detective: Critical Essays on the HBO Series,* ed. Scott F. Stoddart and Michael Samuel. New York: Lexington Books, 2018. 101–16.

Faulkner, William. *Requiem for a Nun.* 1951. New York: Vintage International, 2011.

Feltham, Colin. "The Soul of the Marionette: A Short Enquiry into Human Freedom." *Self and Society* 44, No. 2 (2016): 142–44.

Foley, Richard. "An Epistemology That Matters." philosophy.fas.nyu.edu/docs/IO/1161/epistemologythatmatters.pdf.

Frye, Mitch. "Astonishing Stories: Eudora Welty and the Weird Tale." *Eudora Welty Review* 5 (Spring 2013): 75–93.

Girard, René. *Violence and the Sacred.* Stanford, CA: Stanford University Press, 1978.

Goodreads. "True Detective Reading List." goodreads.com/shelf/show/true-detective-reading-list.

Graham, Jacob, and Tom Sparrow, ed. *True Detective and Philosophy: A Deeper Kind of Darkness*. Hoboken, NJ: John Wiley & Sons, 2018.

Haunted Landscapes: Super-Nature and the Environment. Ed. Ruth Heholt and Niamh Downing. London: Rowman and Littlefield, 2016.

James, Henry. *The Art of Fiction and Other Essays*. New York: Oxford University Press, 1948.

Janning, Finn. "*True Detective*: Pessimism, Buddhism, or Philosophy?" *Journal of Philosophy of Life* 4, No. 4 (2014): 121–41.

Jarvis, Timothy. "The Weird, the Posthuman, and the Abjected World-in-Itself: Fidelity to the 'Lovecraft Event' in the work of Caitlín R. Kiernan and Laird Barron." *Textual Practice* 2017. DOI: 10.1080/0950236X.2017.1358693.

Joshi, S. T. *The Evolution of the Weird Tale*. New York: Hippocampus Press, 2004.

―――. *H. P. Lovecraft: The Decline of the West*. Mercer Island, WA: Starmont House, 1990.

―――. "Lovecraft Criticism: A Study." In *H. P. Lovecraft: Four Decades of Criticism*, ed. S. T. Joshi. Athens: Ohio University Press, 1980. 20–26.

―――. *A Subtler Magick: The Writings and Philosophy of H. P. Lovecraft*. Mercer Island, WA: Starmont House, 1996.

―――. "Thomas Ligotti: The Escape from Life." In *The Modern Weird Tale*. Jefferson, NC: McFarland, 2001. 243–57.

―――. "Why Michel Houellebecq Is Wrong about Lovecraft's Racism." *Lovecraft Annual* No. 12 (2018): 43–50.

―――, and David E. Schultz. *An H. P. Lovecraft Encyclopedia*. Westport, CT: Greenwood Press, 2001.

Joyce, Simon. "Sexual Politics and the Aesthetics of Crime." *English Literary History* 69, No. 2 (Summer 2002): 501–23.

Keen, Suzanne. *Romances of the Archive in Contemporary British Fiction*. Toronto: University of Toronto Press, 2005.

Kellermeyer, M. Grant. "Robert W. Chambers's Surreally Decadent, Nightmarish Horror Stories." www.oldstyletales.com/single-post/2018/02/28/the-brutally-decadent-horror-stories-of-robert-w-chambers-oldstyle-tales-macabre-masters.

Kristeva, Julia. *Powers of Horror: An Essay on Abjection*. New York: Columbia University Press, 2010.

Landrum, Larry N. *American Mystery and Detective Novels: A Reference Guide.* Ed. M. Thomas Inge. Westport, CT: Greenwood Press, 1999.

Lauterbach, Edward. "Some Notes on Cthulhian Pseudobiblia." In *H. P. Lovecraft: Four Decades of Criticism,* ed. S. T. Joshi. Athens: Ohio University Press, 1980. 96–103.

Laws, Robin D. *The Missing and the Lost.* London: Pelgrane Press, 2018.

———. *New Tales of the Yellow Sign.* Alexandria, VA: Atomic Overmind Press, 2018.

Leiber, Fritz, Jr. "A Literary Copernicus." 1949. In *H. P. Lovecraft: Four Decades of Criticism,* ed. S. T. Joshi. Athens: Ohio University Press, 1980. 50–61.

Ligotti, Thomas. *The Conspiracy against the Human Race.* New York: Hippocampus Press, 2010.

———. *Songs of a Dead Dreamer.* 1989. Burton, MI: Subterranean Press, 2010.

Lloyd-Smith, Allan. *American Gothic Fiction: An Introduction.* New York: Continuum International, 2004.

Lovecraft, H. P. *The Annotated Supernatural Horror in Literature.* Ed. S. T. Joshi. Rev. ed. New York: Hippocampus Press, 2012.

———. *Collected Essays.* Ed. S. T. Joshi. New York: Hippocampus Press, 2004–06. 5 vols.

———. *Collected Fiction: A Variorum Edition.* Ed. S. T. Joshi. New York: Hippocampus Press, 2015–17. 4 vols.

———. *Letters to Alfred Galpin and Others.* Ed. S. T. Joshi and David E. Schultz. New York, NY: Hippocampus Press, 2020.

———. *Letters to C. L. Moore and Others.* Ed. David E. Schultz and S. T. Joshi. New York, NY: Hippocampus Press, 2017.

———. *O Fortunate Floridian: H. P. Lovecraft's letters to R. H. Barlow.* Ed. S. T. Joshi and David E. Schultz. Tampa, FL: University of Tampa Press, 2016.

———. *Letters to James F. Morton.* Ed. David E. Schultz and S. T. Joshi. New York, NY: Hippocampus Press, 2011.

———. *Letters to Rheinhart Kleiner and Others.* Ed. S. T. Joshi and David E. Schultz. New York, NY: Hippocampus Press, 2020.

Machin, James. "Music against Horror: H. P. Lovecraft and Schopenhauer's Aesthetics." *East-West Cultural Passage* 1 (2021): 38–50.

———. *Weird Fiction in Britain 1880–1939.* London: Palgrave Macmillan, 2018.

Marshall, Bridget M. "Defining Southern Gothic." In *Critical Insights: Southern Gothic Literature,* ed. Jay Ellis. Ipswich, MA: Salem Press, 2013. 3–18.

Martin, Sean Elliot. "Lovecraft, Absurdity, and the Modernist Grotesque." *Lovecraft Annual* No. 6 (2012): 82–112.

Matthews, J. Barrington. "'Somebody's Memory of a Town': Cary Fukunaga's *True Detective*, Richard Misrach's *Cancer Alley*, and the Posthumanist Landscape." *Athanor* No. 34 (2020): 101–7.

Mencken, H.L. "The Sahara of the Bozart." In *Prejudices: Second Series*. New York: Alfred A. Knopf, 1920. 157–68.

Miller, J. Hillis. "The Critic as Host." *Critical Inquiry* 3, No. 3 (1977): 439–47.

———. "Narrative and History." *ELH* 41, No. 3 (1974): 455–73.

Misrach, Richard and Kate Orff. *Petrochemical America*. New York: Aperture, 2014.

Moghadam, Nahid Shahbazi. "On Placing the Grotesque." *Fantastika Journal* 1, No. 1 (April 2017): 73–90.

Moreland, Sean, ed. *The Lovecraftian Poe: Essays on Influence, Reception, Interpretation and Transformation*. Bethlehem, PA: Lehigh University Press, 2017.

Mosig, Dirk W. "H. P. Lovecraft: Myth-Maker." 1976. In *H. P. Lovecraft: Four Decades of Criticism*, ed. S. T. Joshi. Athens: Ohio University Press, 1980. 104–12.

The New Oxford Annotated Bible: New Revised Standard Version with the Apocrypha. Ed. Michael D. Coogan et al. New York: Oxford University Press, 2018.

O'Connor, Flannery. "Everything That Rises Must Converge." 1965. In *The Complete Stories*. New York: Farrar, Straus & Giroux, 1977. 428–43.

———. "Some Aspects of the Grotesque in Southern Fiction." In *Mystery and Manners: Occasional Prose*. Ed. Sally and Robert Fitzgerald. New York: Farrar, Straus & Giroux, 1969. 36–50.

Pittard, Christopher. *Purity and Contamination in Late Victorian Detective Fiction*. Farnham, UK: Ashgate Publishing, 2011.

Poe, Edgar Allan. "The Murders in the Rue Morgue." 1841. In *The Complete Tales and Poems of Edgar Allan Poe*. New York: Vintage, 1975. 141–68.

———. "The Mystery of Marie Roget." 1842. In *The Complete Tales and Poems of Edgar Allan Poe*. New York: Vintage, 1975. 169–207.

———. "The Purloined Letter." 1844. In *The Complete Tales and Poems of Edgar Allan Poe*. New York: Vintage, 1975. 208–222.

Poirier, Heather. "H. P. Lovecraft and the Dynamics of Detective Fiction." In *Lovecraftian Proceedings 3*, ed. Dennis P. Quinn. New York: Hippocampus Press, 2019. 115–34.

———. "Ripples from Carcosa: H. P. Lovecraft, *True Detective,* and the Artist-Investigator." In *Lovecraftian Proceedings 2,* ed. Dennis P. Quinn. New York: Hippocampus Press, 2017. 208–24.

———. "The Weird within the Real: Common Territories in Lovecraft's Fiction and Southern Literature." In *Lovecraftian Proceedings 4,* ed. Dennis P. Quinn and Elena Tchougounova-Paulson. New York: Hippocampus Press, 2021. 111–25.

Polanski, Roman, dir. *Chinatown.* Paramount, 1974.

Pollard, John. "Depressive Realism: An Existential Response." *Self and Society* 44, No. 2 (2016): 134–41.

Price, Robert M., ed. *The Hastur Cycle.* Oakland, CA: Chaosium, 1993.

Pulver, Joseph S., Sr. *The King in Yellow Tales, Volume 1.* Lovecraft eZine Press, 2015.

Satanis, Venger. "Devotees of Decay and Destruction." *Eldritch Infernal.* web.archive.org/web/20090524061519/http://www.eldritch-infernal.com/ligotti.html.

Sayers, Dorothy L. "Introduction." In *The Omnibus of Crime,* ed. Dorothy L. Sayers. Garden City, NY: Garden City Publishing, 1929. 9–47.

Schweitzer, Darrell. "Eldritch, My Dear Watson." *Sherlock Holmes Mystery Magazine* 4, No. 2 (2018): 19–25.

Setiya, K., and S. T. Joshi. "Lovecraft on Human Knowledge: An Exchange." *Lovecraft Studies* No. 24 (Spring 1991): 22–23, 34.

Sharp, Roberta. "Poe's Duplicitous Dupin." In *Masques, Mysteries, and Mastodons: A Poe Miscellany,* ed. Benjamin F. Fisher. Baltimore: Edgar Allan Poe Society, 2006. 63–76.

Sheedy, Alessandro. "Perverted by Language: Weird Fiction and the Semiotic Anomalies of a Genre." Ph.d. diss.: University of Tasmania, 2016.

Sheehan, Paul, and Lauren Alice. "Labyrinths of Uncertainty: *True Detective* and the Metaphysics of Investigation." *Clues: A Journal of Detection* 35, No. 2 (Fall 2017): 28–39.

Sophocles. *Oedipus the King.* In *The Norton Anthology of World Masterpieces, Volume 1,* ed. Maynard Mack et al. New York: W. W. Norton, 1985. 651–700.

Southwell, David. "Hookland: Folklore, Landscape Punk, and Psychogeography." folklorethursday.com/creative-corner/970/.

Spiegel, Alan. "A Theory of the Grotesque in Southern Fiction." *Georgia Review* 26, No. 4 (Winter 1972): 426–37.

Trigg, Dylan. "Horror." *International Lexicon of Aesthetics,* Spring 2020. DOI: 10.7413/18258630088.

True Detective. Created and written by Nic Pizzolatto. HBO, 2014. Amazon Prime Video, amazon.com/Amazon-Video.

Walsh, Christopher J. "'Dark Legacy': Gothic Ruptures in Southern Literature." In *Critical Insights: Southern Gothic Literature,* ed. Jay Ellis. Ipswich, MA: Salem Press, 2013. 19–34.

Weech, Edward. "Light versus Dark: Truth and Transcendence in *True Detective.*" Electricghost.co.uk/light-versus-dark-truth-transcendence-in-true-detective.

Welty, Eudora. "Place in Fiction." In *The Eye of the Story: Selected Essays and Reviews.* New York: Vintage, 1978. 116–33.

Wikipedia. "Palimpsest." en.wikipedia.org/wiki/Palimpsest.

Woodard, Ben. "Mad Speculation and Absolute Inhumanism: Lovecraft, Ligotti, and the Weirding of Philosophy." *Continent* 1, No. 1 (2011): 3–13.

Zapffe, Peter Wessel. "The Last Messiah." 1933. Tr. Gisele R. Tangenes. philosophynow.org/issues/45/The_Last_Messiah.

Zeegers, Nicolle. "What Epistemology Would Serve Criminal Law Best in Finding the Truth about Rape?" *Law and Method.* www.bjutijdschriften.nl/tijdschrift/lawandmethod/2012/1/ReM_2212-2508_2012_002_001_005.

Index

abjection 10, 56, 101; and Lovecraft 110–11
aesthetic(s) 10, 21, 57, 113; and Chambers, 23, chapter 2, 68–69, 70; and crime, 71–72, 75; and detective fiction tropes, 93; and epistemology, 43, 44, 71; and the grotesque, 108; and investigation, chapter 4; 43, 64, 70, 71, 72; and Lovecraft, 43, 70; and masking, 21; and Poe, 70, 71; and redemption, 71, 72; and tabletop role-playing games, 36; and *True Detective,* 34, 72–73, 75–76
Bakhtin, Mikhail 107–8
Bierce, Ambrose 10, 32, 113
Budden, Gary 10, 16
Burleson, Donald R. 19, 20, 24–25
Call of Cthulhu (tabletop role-playing game [TTRPG]) 36; *Ripples from Carcosa* (TTRPG), 36; *Tatters of the King* (TTRPG), 36
Cancer Alley 13, 17, 37, 114–15
Carcosa 10, 17–18, 23–27, chapter 2, 113, 115, 120; and *Impossible Landscapes,* 37; and Lovecraft, 45; *New Tales of the Yellow Sign / The Missing and the Lost,* 38; *Ripples from Carcosa* (TTRPG), 36
Chambers, Robert W. 7, 9–10, 14, 15–16, chapter 2, 113; aesthetics of, 68–70; and deconstruction, 26; and eschatology, 23; investigation in, 61, 68; landscape in, 12, 14–15, 115; and masks, 21, 24, 68; and metonymy, 24; and narrative, 25–26; and tropes, 16; and *True Detective,* chapter 4, chapter 7
Christie, Agatha 62–63, 82
Cohle, Rustin 13, 14–15, 24, 72, 118–19, 121–23; aesthetic sensibilities of, 42, 59, 69, 75–76; as Copernicus, 74–75; and epistemology, 120–22; and investigation, 65, 73–75, 77–78, 125; and Ligotti, 59–60, 117, 120; and locked room, 34; and masks, 24; and palimpsest, 73–74; and pessimism, 16, 60, 117–18; and The Play, 74; and time, 23
cosmic horror 13, 14, 19, 22–24, 36–38, 40, 41, 43, 50–51, 56–58, 62, 65–67, 69, 76–77, 79, 88–89, 91–94, 96–97, 105, chapter 6, chapter 7
Courir de Mardi Gras 16–17
Conspiracy against the Human Race, The. See Ligotti, Thomas
Cult of the Yellow King 15, 24, 26, 75, chapter 7
criminal 9, 14, 35, 64, 93; and aesthetics, 72; and criminality, 10, 71, 82, 92; and the detective, 61–63, 91, 118, 124; and epistemological order, 84, 85, 88–89; and investigation, 71, 72; and narrative, 65, 68, 72; and redemption, 72; and the tri-

partite dynamic, 63, 89–90, 92; and violence, 90

Decadent(s) chapter 2, 70

deconstruction 10, 12, chapter 1, 67

Delta Green (TTRPG) 17, 26, 36, 38

detective fiction 10, chapter 4, chapter 5, 113, 118–19; aesthetics of, 43; and deconstruction, 21, 25; and the detective, 42; and narrative, 124; and normative values, 10; and tropes, 14

Dhammapada 53

Doyle, Sir Arthur Conan 10, 61, 71, 80, 81, 86; in Cannon, 91; in Schweitzer, 87

epistemology 10, 21, 23, 27, chapter 2, 50, 54–55, 64, 70–71, 84–85, 88–89, 108, 113, 120–22, 124

espionage fiction 63

Faulkner, William 9, 14, 24, chapter 6, 101, 102, 119, 120, 124; and Lovecraft, 103, 104; and the grotesque, 108, 112; *Requiem for a Nun*, 12; "A Rose for Emily," 99; *The Sound and the Fury*, 108; and the Southern Renaissance, 103; Yoknapatawpha County, 102

figure (*literary*) 10

Girard, René 63, 84, 88; and mimetic violence, 90; and ritual violence, 89–90, 123; and tripartite dynamic, 88, 91–92; *Violence and the Sacred*, 89–91

Gothic 72, 80, 83; American, 11, 101, 105; European, 11, 105; and Lovecraft, 86–87; and race, 81–82; Southern, 10, 11, 24, 64, chapter 6, 113, 119

grotesque 10, chapter 6, 113, 119, 124; as aesthetic category, 108–9

Hart, Martin 14, 24, 59–60, chapter 4, 118–19, 120–23, 125

haunted landscape(s) chapter 1, 10, 15, 21, 115, 118–19, 124–25; and ghosts, 13, 15

Holmes, Sherlock 62, 71, 80, 81, 82, 86, 87, 91, 94

Impossible Landscapes (TTRPG) 17–18, 26, 36–38, 120

Joshi, S. T. 50, 76, 87–88, 92

King in Yellow, The (Chambers) chapter 2, 9, 113; the Book 9, 10, 12, 14–16, chapter 2, chapter 4, 113; Hildred Castaigne, 14–15, chapter 2, 120, 125; "The Mask," chapter 2, 68; "The Repairer of Reputations," 14, chapter 2, 125; "The Yellow Sign," chapter 2; the Play, 9, 15, 22, 23–26, 27, chapter 4, 74, 113, 115; the Yellow King, 15–17, 22–27, chapter 2, 69, 74–75, chapter 7, 117

Kristeva, Julia 110–11

Lange, Dora 7, 22, 60, 61, 75, 118, 121, 128

landscape punk 10, 16, 18

landscape studies 12

Leiber, Fritz 74–75, 117

Ligotti, Thomas chapter 3, 9, 113, chapter 7; *The Conspiracy against the Human Race*, chapter 3, 116–17; and the Dhammapada, 10, 53; four limitations on human consciousness, 48; "The Last Messiah," 48; and the locked room of the mind, chapter 3; 34; and Lovecraft, 56–59, 116–18; and Rustin Cohle, 10, 59–60, 119, 120, 122

Louisiana 9, 12, 14, 15, 17, 24, 66, 73, 75, 88, chapter 7

Lovecraft, H. P. 9, 10, 12–13, 24, 113, 123, 124–25; aesthetic sensibilities of, 35, 42–43, chapter 4; *At the Mountains of Madness*, 14, 69, 75–76, 92, 94, 105, 111; "Beyond the Wall of Sleep," 104; "The Call of

Cthulhu," 66, 86, 87, 88, 105; and Carcosa, 45; and Robert W. Chambers, 30, 32, 34, 125; and cosmic horror, 13, 15, 39, 41, 115–16; and detective fiction, chapter 5; "The Dreams in the Witch House," 94; "The Dunwich Horror," 66–67, 104; and the grotesque, 112; "The Horror at Red Hook," 82, 87; and landscape 14, 15–17, 18; and Ligotti, chapter 3, 116–17; "The Music of Erich Zann," 43, 69; and narrative, 26–27; "Pickman's Model," 69–70; "The Picture in the House," 92, 111–12; "The Rats in the Walls," 95, 106; and realism, 19, 21, 22, 25, 106–7; and return of the repressed, 106; and sense of place, 13, 101; "The Shadow out of Time," 79, 92, 96–97; "The Shadow over Innsmouth," 104; "The Shunned House," 87; and Southern literature, 15, chapter 6; "The Statement of Randolph Carter," 86; "Supernatural Horror in Literature," 45, 74, 80–81, 83–84, 86–87; and teleology, 23; "The Thing on the Doorstep," 92; and *True Detective*, 118–20, 122; "The Whisperer in Darkness," 95, 123

mask(s) and masking. *See* trope(s)

Miller, J. Hillis 10, chapter 1; "Narrative and History," 18–23, 25–27

mimesis chapter 5

Missing and the Lost, The (Laws) 38–39, 120

Neuromancer (Gibson) 40

New Tales of the Yellow Sign (Laws) 38, 120

O'Connor, Flannery chapter 6, 124; "Everything That Rises Must Converge," 109–11; "Good Country People," 107; "A Good Man Is Hard to Find," 109; and the grotesque, 105, 108–9, 112; and mystery, 107; pessimism in, 120

palimpsest(s). *See* trope(s)

Petrochemical America (Misrach and Orff) 9, 10, 17, 114; and landscape punk, 18; and *Impossible Landscapes*, 37

Pizzolatto, Nic 34, 59, 117

Poe, Edgar Allan 9, 10, 24, 33, 35, 101, 113; and aesthetics of investigation, 70; and abjection, 101; and detective fiction, 61, 81; and epistemological order, 84; "The Fall of the House of Usher," 101; and Lovecraft, 83; "The Mystery of Marie Rogêt," 64–65, 84–85

Pulver, Joseph S., Sr. 30, 35

puppet 34, 39, chapter 3, 76, 118, 121

question to answer, the 10, 113

redemption 23, 31, 33, 38, 40, 71–72, 94, 115

revelation and concealment. *See* trope(s)

ritual violence 89–90, 123

Schopenhauer, Arthur 47, 52, 55, 57, 117; and Indian mysticism, 54

sense of place 22, 101, 102; in Lovecraft, 13, 15, 106

Setiya, K. 50

South (the American) 14, chapter 6, 119; and Lovecraft, chapter 6; power structures, 17, 121–22, 124; and Southern history, 12, 17, 122; violence in culture, 122–24

Southern literature 10, 12, 15, chapter 6, 113, 119; grotesque in, 124; haunted landscapes in, 23; Southern Gothic (*see* Gothic); Southern Renaissance, 103–4; and *True Detective*, 22–23, 120–21

Southwell, David 10, 16

structuralism 20, 67; and post-structuralism, 20–21, 25

tabletop role-playing games (TTRPGs). *See individual titles and systems*
teleology 23, 27, 54, 70, 88
tripartite dynamics 63, 89, 91–92
trope(s) 10, chapter 5, 101; amateur and professional, 93; below, in Southern literature, 100; clarity and obscurity, 64, 92; darkness and light, 64; doubling, 33, 41; guilt and confession, 93; masking and unmasking, 10, 21, 41, 68, 92, 95; mirroring, 33, 40; narrative struggle for dominance, 64, 65, 124; palimpsest(s), 10, 13, 16, 64, 73–74, 93, 94–95, 120; presence and absence, 64; private and public, 93; revelation and concealment, 10, 20–21, 68, 85, 88–89, 92–94, 95; sin and atonement, 93; truth and deceit, 93; woundedness, 38, 41, 115–16
True Detective 9–10, chapter 4, 112, 113, chapter 7; and Robert W. Chambers, 16, chapter 2, 26; and eschatology, 23–24; and the haunted, 21; and the grotesque, 10; and landscape, 10, 12, 14–17; and Ligotti, chapter 3; and Lovecraft, chapter 4; masking in, 21–22, 24; and metonymy, 24–25; and *Petrochemical America,* 17, 115; realism in, 25; and social structures, 24; and Southern history, 15, 17; and Southern literature, 23; and the Yellow King, 16, 22, 24, 25–27, 118; S1E1 "The Long Bright Dark," 13, 75–76; S1E2 "Seeing Things," 121; S1E3 "The Locked Room," 62, 75, 76, 77, 78, 125; S1E4 "Who Goes There," 118; S1E5 "The Secret Fate of All Life," 73–74, 77; S1E6 "Haunted Houses," 122; S1E7 "After You're Gone," 26, 76, 77; S1E8 "Form and Void," 77, 128

unreal cartographies 102–3

Violence and the Sacred (Girard). See Girard, René

weird fiction 10, 16, 22, 26, 39, 59, 117, 120; and Robert W. Chambers, 29–30; and detective fiction, 68, 80, 86, 92; and Edgar Allan Poe, 83; and Southern literature, chapter 6; and *True Detective,* 61; and Wagner, Karl Edward, 35–36

Welty, Eudora 13, 101, 102, 124

Williams, Tennessee 124

Zapffe, Peter Wessel chapter 3; 117

www.ingramcontent.com/pod-product-compliance
Lightning Source LLC
Chambersburg PA
CBHW071124090426
42736CB00012B/2006